MARICOPA COUNT
SOUTH MOUNTAIN
SOUTH MOUNTAIN
7050 SOUTH 24TH STREET
PHOENIX, AZ 85042

M000159171

DISCARDED

The Power of Customer Misbehavior

The Power of Customer Misbehavior

Drive Growth and Innovation by Learning from Your Customers

Michael Fisher, Martin Abbott, and Kalle Lyytinen

First published 2014 by
PALGRAVE MACMILLAN

Palgrave Macmillan in the UK is an imprint of Macmillan Publishers Limited, registered in England, company number 785998, of Houndmills, Basingstoke, Hampshire RG21 6XS.

Palgrave Macmillan in the US is a division of St Martin's Press LLC, 175 Fifth Avenue, New York, NY 10010.

Palgrave Macmillan is the global academic imprint of the above companies and has companies and representatives throughout the world.

Palgrave® and Macmillan® are registered trademarks in the United States, the United Kingdom, Europe and other countries.

ISBN 978–1–137–34891–3

This book is printed on paper suitable for recycling and made from fully managed and sustained forest sources. Logging, pulping and manufacturing processes are expected to conform to the environmental regulations of the country of origin.

A catalogue record for this book is available from the British Library.

A catalog record for this book is available from the Library of Congress.

Typeset by MPS Limited, Chennai, India.

Contents

	Figures and Tables	vi
	Acknowledgments	viii
	Introduction	1
1	Why is Viral Growth Important?	17
2	Technological Factors	34
3	The Viral Model	46
4	The Concept of Self-Identity	61
5	Identity and Self-Verification	68
6	Seeing and Being Seen	82
7	Getting it Right	98
8	Getting it Wrong	116
9	Conclusion	130

Appendix A: Viral Growth	143
Appendix B: A Short Summary of Research Informing the Book Findings	146
Glossary	160
Notes and References	162
Index	185

Figures and Tables

Figures

1.1	Google Search for 'Honey Badger'	18
1.2	US City Populations	21
1.3	Viral Growth Equation	24
1.4	Tupperware vs. Rubbermaid Stock	29
1.5	Amplification Growth – http://afkpartners.com	31
2.1	S-Curve	36
2.2	Bell Curve	37
2.3	Technology Adoption Lifecycle Groups	38
2.4	Technology Acceptance Model	42
3.1	Virtuous Cycle of Customer Misbehavior	51
3.2	Partial Model	55
3.3	Extended Model	57
5.1	Drivers of Viral Growth	74
5.2	Drivers of Viral Growth with Feedback	78, 95, 139
7.1	Facebook Growth	101
7.2	Hashtag Example	106
7.3	Zynga Stock from 31 Aug 2012 to 8 Apr 2013	110
7.4	Google Trends for 'Silly String'	112
9.1	Salesforce.com Subscriber Growth	132
A.1	Overall Research Design	148
A.2	Triangulation Mixed Method Research Model	149
A.3	Structural Model	157

Tables

9.1	How to Make Use of the Model	141
A.1	Original and Selected Themes	151
A.2	Confirmatory Factor Analysis Results, Correlations, and Reliability	153
A.3	Model Fit Statistics for Structural Analysis	155

Acknowledgments

Every research project and every book is supported by a cast of many – especially projects such as this book, which required people to give their time for personal interviews. We would like to acknowledge the commitment by Intuit executives Laura Fennell, Troy Otillio, and Tayloe Stansbury in discussing their stories of Live Community and making the time within their busy schedules to share the Intuit story. We'd also like to thank Simon Rothman for his eBay Motors story and Maryrose Dunton for her many stories about YouTube in the early years.

We would also like to thank Dick Boland, Case Western Reserve University, and Toni Somers and Sheri Perelli from Wayne State University for comments and ideas around the concept of viral growth. Additionally we would also like to thank the members of the Doctor of Management Program cohort 2013 for their feedback and comments on the earlier drafts of the research.

The underlying research that this book is based on has taken years to develop and great amounts of time away from our families. The authors would like to acknowledge the sacrifice that each of our families has made in order for this research and book to be completed. Without their patience, support, and encouragement we would not have endured.

Lastly we would like to thank all the talented and professional individuals at Palgrave Macmillan. They have been staunch supporters of this project from the beginning, seeing the value of having this research widely distributed for students, fellow researchers, and practitioners.

Introduction

MISBEHAVING CUSTOMERS AND PRODUCT MISUSE AS A SOURCE OF COMPANY GROWTH?

In many ways, Simon Rothman was a typical young executive. Having graduated with an MBA from Harvard Business School in 1995, he joined McKinsey & Company, a high-end strategy consulting firm, and rose quickly to the position of Engagement Manager. In 1998, the allure of the Internet and related new ways of doing business brought Simon to the Silicon Valley. After leaving the buttoned-down and comparatively safe confines of McKinsey, Simon toiled around the Valley for a while, eventually joining eBay – a fast growing Internet company soon to conduct an IPO – as a strategist in the business and corporate development team. Simon's task was to create new relationships and generate new revenue streams with corporate partners.

In 1998, eBay was still highly focused on being an online marketplace for collectible items: PEZ™ dispensers, Beanie Babies, model vehicles, and the like. eBay carried no inventory and had nothing to sell of its own. It was the equivalent of an online 'flea market' – a virtual place where buyers and sellers could meet and exchange goods – but only through an auction-based protocol. The company was still young, having been started in 1995 by Pierre Omidyar in his San Jose, CA living room. By 1998 the company had net revenues of $47.4 million, up from $5.7 million the prior year. This incredible 724 per cent increase in revenues was one of the reasons Simon was interested in joining the company and learning about its new online business model.

Simon was a car enthusiast, and his cubicle at eBay was festooned with collectible model cars. One day, while searching through eBay for a toy Burrago Ferrari 365, he stumbled across a seller who was claiming to be selling a *real* Ferrari. In those days the press was full of stories of people trying to sell body parts, internal organs, and even their virginity on eBay. The highest priced item that had yet sold on the site was a very collectible Beanie Baby for near $20,000. In some cases, fraudsters attempted to use the online trading platform to take advantage of other people with fake or non-existent goods or services. In Simon's mind, this was more likely to be a joke, a fraudulent listing, or perhaps even a confused seller. Simon decided he had to call the seller to find out what was going on.

The seller of the Ferrari appeared to be legitimate. His wife was an avid eBay fan and together they lived in a rural community – one that simply could not generate enough demand to create a market for such a luxury car. The car, reasoned the seller, was a collectible and eBay was a site dedicated to the buying and selling of collectible items. Given the choice of the local market with relatively low demand and a product built to buy and sell collectibles (albeit collectibles of lower value than the car), the seller chose eBay. With a bit more searching, Simon turned up other similar examples of real collectible vehicles for sale on the site. While there was little evidence of buyers purchasing these vehicles, it was clear to Simon that there might be an opportunity to create a marketplace where collectible vehicles could in fact be bought and sold.

Before continuing the story of what actions Simon took, based on this discovery of a real car being sold on eBay, it is important to understand the state of the used car market in the late 1990s. Used car sales were becoming big business, with retail dealerships selling more than twice the number of used cars as new cars (20.5 million used vs. 8.8 million new).[1] The average selling price of a used car grew from $5800 in the early 1990s, to roughly $8000 in 1999. This significant increase in price meant that more used cars were financed when purchased and that more used cars had liens remaining on them when being sold. Selling a car with a lien against its title can be a complex transaction for an individual to handle. Retail dealerships represented both a faster path for buyers who might need financing help and for sellers who had a lien remaining on their vehicle. As a result, dealerships captured a majority of the market for used car sales, driving private (outside of dealership) sales of used cars down by nearly 50 per cent in the 1990s.[2]

These trends indicated to most people that the addressable market for private sales of used cars was shrinking. Furthermore, the eBay site at the time wasn't well equipped to handle the private sales of cars. Buyers didn't have an easy way to identify important attributes of a vehicle such as the year, model, make, mileage, or location of the sale. While the seller could add these attributes in unformatted fields, the job of searching for them by a potential buyer could be considered onerous at best. Present-day users of modern commerce sites (including eBay) have grown accustomed to specialized searches that allow buyers to search for items by size, color, and a number of other product attributes. Few, if any, of these capabilities were available on eBay at the time. Searches were performed either against the title of an item or a combination of the title and description of the listings for sale on the site. Finding a red Ford Mustang with fewer than 50,000 miles on the odometer may have taken several attempts and returned only a small number of the actual vehicles. If the desired vehicle was outside a buyer's local area, the buyer needed to figure out a way with the seller to secure the vehicle after the sale. Finally, the fees that sellers paid to sell large items like automobiles would be significantly higher than alternatives like the classified section of their local newspaper or periodicals specializing in person-to-person car sales. The eBay platform charged a 'final value fee' – a percentage of the final sale price of the auction, as compared to classified ads that would typically charge a flat fee, based on duration and size of the ad. The difference for sales of vehicles like high-end collector cars could be hundreds or even thousands of dollars.

Clearly with a shrinking addressable market and a platform completely unsuited (at the time) for such transactions, the selling of 'real' vehicles was either something to be ignored or perhaps even squelched. After all, eBay would not want to be held responsible for transactions that went poorly, especially when its current product could not adequately support the specific needs of those transactions. Ample research and practical experiences on effective management and strategy teach us that this is exactly how most managers are trained and even expected to approach such a new finding. Companies and managers need to stay focused on their current market segment or service and seek to aggressively grow in that segment through price-cutting, competitively differentiated products, and so on. They should not attempt to change their focus or product mix by yielding easily to the varying needs of potential customers. Such changes increase the cost of products, make products more complex, and demand too much managerial attention. In addition, executives finding the activities of 'lead users' using their product in new and innovative ways are likely to underestimate the market and revenue possibility of such usage.[3] It is easy to come to the conclusion that such lead user behaviors are a nuisance: an instance of misbehaving customers who seek to misuse the current product and distract management from executing their strategic plan. eBay was no better suited to sell automobiles in 1998 than a cell phone is designed to be used as a hammer. Most conventional managers would ignore or shut down the actions of these misbehaving customers and focus on returning to, and dominating, their initial target market.

While Simon may have ostensibly appeared to be the conventional and well-educated entrepreneurial executive on an accelerated career path, his actions were anything but what research indicates is typical of executives in similar positions. While research indicates most executives would ignore the sales of collectible cars on eBay, Simon decided to enable it. Where most executives would erect barriers to stop such activity on the site, Simon decided instead to enable this behavior by reducing the friction for these types of transactions. In so doing he helped create one of eBay's largest and fastest growing categories, as measured by total merchandise sales, and revolutionize a portion of the used automobile market.

Simon's task was not an easy one. eBay was an innovative startup that prided itself on its ability to identify and enable the selling of new product categories on its site. But many executives viewed the used car market as simply too small, and the investment to support it too large. To many, the investment seemed too risky with too low a probability of an appropriately sized return on investment. eBay, in those days, spent its product development effort and capital on features and functionality that could be leveraged across multiple product categories related to collectibles. The notion of customizing the eBay product for a single category like vehicles was foreign to the prevailing investment logic. Research shows that most companies behave this way – preferring research and development or product development approaches that serve multiple segments over specialized offerings specific to any single market segment. Innovation is sourced internally through research and development groups rather than seeking opportunities for innovation from existing activities within their market segments.[4] The reason for the dominance of internal approaches is easy to explain. In order to make sense of the business environment in which most companies compete, executives need to become adept at using processes and models that help reduce and make sense of the vast stream of market information. The resulting reliance on common, established approaches invites companies to kill, or approach with suspicion, customer-led innovation.[5] The very approach that makes them successful for the common customer case becomes a barrier that prevents them from identifying and making use of new innovations on their products created by their own customers.

Simon's eBay Motors experience is emblematic of the reasons we felt a need to write this book. His story highlights the spectrum of innovative behaviors that, for the lack of a better term, managers often call 'misuse' or 'customer misbehavior'. This is not the same as customer-based fraud or customers seeking to benefit from the company by using questionable methods or practices. We would indeed be remiss if we did not admit that customers do misbehave, attempting to take advantage of a company and their products. People do use products for nefarious or ethically questionable purposes. Payment fraud is an example of one such type of misbehavior, where fraudsters attempt to use a payment platform to purchase goods with someone else's money. PayPal's (an eBay company) exploration and early identification of this value-destroying misuse, and the resulting response, helps keep its customers safe from fraudsters with one of the lowest fraud rates of any payment service. One of the main questions that we will explore in this book is: given most companies' tendency to view all usage outside of the original intent as 'bad', how do we identify value-creating 'good' misbehavior?

In the example above, we can see that customer's misuse involves a situation where a customer behaves in ways that go against some management assumptions about appropriate customer behaviors in relation to the current products. This is a situation where managers do not have good ways of making sense of such behavior and knowing how to respond to it. 'Misbehavior' and 'misuse' are hubristic terms that paint management as having greater intelligence about markets and customers than the customers have in using the products. 'Misuse' and 'customer misbehavior' are thus unfortunate terms that fail to account for the alternative ways in which customers may make sense of, and give meaning to, our products.[6] The use of these terms is forced upon us by the limitations of the English language: we do not have good words (at least in our experience) to distinguish between nefarious usage and usage that expands or extends product capabilities.

Whereas 'misuse' seems to close the door on strategic options and predestine us to shut down potentially innovative behavior, the French term *bricolage* eliminates the pejorative connation and leaves the door open for strategic options. Bricolage means to use an item or object for a purpose other than its intended one. Bricolage leaves us open to interpreting unforeseen usage as a possible extension to our product, as something that we might enable and celebrate rather than disable and neglect. Bricolage opens the door to us viewing our products as something that we produce with our customers, rather than just for our customers. Throughout this book we will repeatedly use the terms 'misbehavior' and 'misuse' to help remind us of the limitations we put on ourselves as we explore some of the unfortunate decisions made by companies we follow and study in this book. We will use the term 'bricolage' occasionally, to help us return to the more open-minded and positive approach that we argue for in this book in examining unforeseen uses of product. This latter approach is the one we hope our readers will adopt.

This book is about the nature, causes, and effects of customer misbehaviors – a.k.a. bricolage – that are innovative in nature. By innovative we mean a range of behaviors that is original in that it has not occurred before, and unique in that it is not common among the typical uses of the products. For example, the original intended use of eBay was to create and expand a marketplace for 'collectible' things that previously had no easily accessible market. Pierre Omidyar did not initially envision the sales of vehicles but neither did his vision preclude them as one possible way of using the product. Simon and his team's actions in identifying, enabling, and supporting unexpected behavior created significant value for both eBay's customers and for shareholders.

THE JOURNEY TO MISUSE AS A SOURCE OF GROWTH

The authors have researched and/or worked at both Fortune 500 companies and technology startups for over 20 years. While we have been fortunate to actually benefit from enabling customer misbehaviors at companies like eBay, we were blind to this phenomenon because of the lack of a language available to identify, analyze, and discuss it. Whatever success the authors personally had was dumb luck rather than the result of mindful, purposeful action to identify and enable such customer-led innovation. But over the last three to four years, as a result of reflection and careful academic scrutiny, we slowly came to understand this phenomenon and its importance.

This journey started in 2009 when Mike Fisher prepared an initial research proposal that led a few years later to his doctoral dissertation. Mike was intrigued by how two companies that started at roughly the same time with similar ideas (Facebook and Friendster) emerged in a few years with two completely different results. Facebook achieved viral growth and incredible success while Friendster met with (comparatively) spectacular failure. The term 'viral' is quite possibly one of the most overused and misunderstood words in the English language. From a biological perspective, it almost always has a negative connotation given its association with the spreading of various diseases. In the business world, it is something that companies, both young and old, desire to achieve with their products and marketing efforts. The problem is that the word is used (and misused) so often, by so many people referring to so many events that its meaning is at best diluted and at worst completely lost. The term 'viral growth' is often used to describe exponential growth patterns of products or services that are comparable to the spread of a contagious virus in a population. While the adoption of new products has been described rhetorically with the term 'contagion' for centuries,[7] 'contagion' has been coined recently to characterize the fast spread in the use of Internet-based platform services, such as social networking sites like Facebook and Friendster.[8] We'll cover more about the concept of viral growth and why companies would like to achieve it in Chapter 1.

The initial paths taken by Facebook and Friendster were arguably different. Friendster became a household name early on in Silicon Valley, while Facebook was primarily used by young students attending Ivy League Universities. Facebook was definitely a 'viral' phenomenon, beginning life as Facemash, a 'hot or not' comparison game that allowed Harvard students to compare two student pictures and vote for those who were 'hot' and those who were 'not'. From its launch as Facemash on 28 October 2003 to its initial public offering in 2012, Facebook grew to over one billion active users.[9] By any objective measure, Facebook is a shining example of viral success. But are all companies or products that go 'viral' successful?

Friendster also achieved viral success after its launch in May of 2002[10] and reached three million users within just a handful of months. Myspace, another social media site, was founded in 2003, and between 2005 to early 2006 was one of the most visited social networking sites in the world.[11] Both of these companies clearly experienced viral growth and some measure of success at some point in time. But neither company experienced the same degree of success as Facebook. Whereas Facebook's public market capitalization (the total value of all of its issued shares or equity) was greater than $100 billion at its initial public offering, Friendster was sold to a Malaysian company in 2009 for $26.9 million and Myspace sold to a media group including Justin Timberlake for $35 million in 2011.[12] In the years of their sales, Myspace had fallen to be the 133rd most trafficked Internet site in the

US, and Friendster was primarily a site focusing on the Asian market with 115 million active users.

Mike suspected that something unusual and important could explain the surprising success of Facebook and the as equally surprising failure of Friendster. As is the case with many doctoral journeys, his initial findings were unexpected and completely inconsistent with his initial expectations; they begged for further analysis. Interviews with executives and users of many social networking sites unearthed a common phenomenon in the sites that were successful – a phenomenon that was completely absent in the failed companies. And, this was not about sharpness and soundness of business models, technological capability and ambition, or quality of leadership. The explanation was quite different and related to how these sites learned from, and perhaps more importantly *with*, 'misbehaving' customers.

Social networking sites are designed to allow users to create, share, and consume *their personal* content. Academics refer to this creation and consumption of content as the *co-creation of value*.[13] Because social networking sites exist to enable one to share content within one's social network, the scope and level of co-creation is highly correlated with the viral growth of such sites. Sites that effectively enable and promote higher levels of co-creation appear to exhibit greater viral growth. In social networks, users co-create when they add their status updates, produce original content, add photos or links to content, or consume or leave comments (such as 'like it!') on similar content produced by people within their 'networks'. Without this user activity a social network becomes hollow and is of no value to the potential users. Without new people joining to consume the content, or consume more content, there is little reason for others to produce the content. While both social networking sites were initially quite similar in the range and volume of co-creation, they differed quite dramatically in how their users innovated. The level of user innovation appeared to vary with the amount of freedom afforded the users by management to 'misuse' the product or 'misbehave'.

A user's engagement in the actual definition or creation of a product or service itself is known in academic literature as *co-production*.[14] Co-production happens when a firm and its customers learn to work together in the definition, development, implementation, and evolution of the firm's product or service. An extreme case of co-production is the case of 'misuse', where customers co-produce on a product in ways not originally expected, and potentially even *against* the original design intent of the firm offering the product. Consider, for example, Simon Rothman's identification that someone was indeed attempting to sell a real Ferrari within the model Ferrari section of eBay. In this case eBay was acting much like a social network; sellers and buyers co-created value through the production of content (items for sale on eBay) and the consumption of that content (people bidding on the items for sale). The seller of the *real* Ferrari was, however, moved beyond co-creation into co-production: he used the product and associated business processes in a new and unique way to meet his own specific needs.

Fascinating stories of innovation, enthusiasm, growth, and changes in company strategy and execution emerge when companies identify and leverage product misuse. In fact, most successful companies in the fast growing Web 2.0 or social networking arena did exactly what eBay did – they learned quickly to actively identify new and unusual usage and then worked to enable it, to promote it and learn to derive value from it. As a result, customers in fact turbo-charged the growth of these sites – they helped firms to both develop and market their products for free. The less successful companies mostly ignored it and only acknowledged its value occasionally when the evidence was totally obvious. The least successful companies, in contrast, attempted to block such behavior.

Analysis of thousands of user and employee surveys supports our interview findings: the identification and enabling of misuse, where it is neither legally or ethically restricted, nor controlled by government regulation, correlates highly with firm growth and success in social networking sites. We then wondered whether this discovery applied to other Internet-enabled industries and, further, whether we could find evidence outside Internet services in the broader technology market. To our surprise, the story grew larger and we were able to find other examples of customer innovation masquerading as customer misbehavior. Customers across several industries were actually misbehaving and co-producing (misusing) products! As we analyzed these stories of product misuse it became clear to us that they painted a picture of a constantly changing and dynamic world – a world in which the innovating consumer, and not the innovating company, is now king. In this new world, successful companies need to follow and identify customer innovations and then move quickly to enable those innovations. Companies continuing to operate in the old world, where feature sets are dictated to customers based on internal innovation, will quickly find themselves marginalized and incapable of competing against their faster-moving brethren. Successful companies will eagerly watch their customers misuse their products and services and embark upon a cooperative journey of learning and exploration. The most successful companies will build products with the understanding that co-production is likely, desirable, and often necessary. These companies will have designed their services to both allow for a broad range of misuse and to identify and report such misuse as it happens.

The cycle of searching for customer innovation and misbehavior in new and innovative ways, followed by the enablement of that behavior, becomes the force that turns the crank that drives the gears of growth. The tighter the cycle of innovation, the faster the crank turns, and the greater the potential for growth. But a cycle of innovation without a mechanism against which it can be employed is not very useful. Stories that illustrate how companies seek innovation from customers might be useful, but even more useful is to know how to create products that incent customer interaction and co-creation and how to create mechanisms that foster learning from misuse.

WHY DO CUSTOMERS 'MISBEHAVE' WITH OUR PRODUCTS?

The ideas that customer misbehavior is valuable and that identifying and enabling it can fuel growth are, we argue, the table stakes in the new world order. But to reach the pinnacle of success, companies need to build products that lend themselves to vast and varied uses and misuses. To do so we must understand the reasons why customers are motivated to use products in new and innovative ways, and the context within which such usage emerges. To that end, we need to ask two questions:

1. Why do users initially use a firm's products?

2. What causes customers to misbehave and misuse (i.e. co-produce) those products?

In a seminal 1989 paper, Fred Davis described two antecedents to adoption of IT products – *perceived ease of use* and *perceived usefulness*.[15] Perceived usefulness speaks to the customer's need for the product to have some initial perceived utility – that it solves some problem for them or fills some identified need. Perceived ease of use indicates the effort the user needs to exert to learn and use the product. The higher the effort the less likely it is that most customers will adopt the service. The more easy to use a product is, the higher the probability of adoption. The word 'perceived' is important here, as the constructs that Davis suggests are psychometric in nature – they explain how customers will 'see' or 'experience' the product – they do not describe the actual ease of use or utility of the product relative to other products or on an absolute basis.

Davis' theory states that the higher the user's perceived usefulness the greater the likelihood of product adoption. Similarly, the more the customer sees that the product is easy to use, the more willing the customer is to adopt the product.[16] These two concepts form the base of what we will call our pyramid of viral growth, which we will cover in detail in Chapter 3. Before a product can achieve such hyper-growth, it must by definition be adopted by customers; without adoption we have no base from which to grow user base.

The reason why customers misbehave and start to misuse products took us a bit more time to derive. Clearly, as Simon's story at eBay indicates, at least one reason why customers innovate by misbehaving is to create new economic value that they can share. For example, the Ferrari owner wanted to sell his car for a reasonable price and in so doing extended the perceived usefulness of eBay. We may also find ourselves in need of a hammer to hang a picture, but only have a cell phone on hand to tap in the nail. Other examples may include using a pen knife as a screw driver, or using the tip of a ball point pen to help remove packing tape from a box.

However our research into social networking sites, and interviews with users and executives, hinted at another less obvious driver of customer misbehaviors that resulted in product misuse. Unlike the eBay story, participants in most social network sites are not involved in an exercise of creating joint economic utility. In contrast, our interviews indicated that the users were often involved in a process of defining or sometimes redefining themselves online. The questions we asked them were meant to elicit stories of their interactions and related 'perceived usefulness', but their responses were often personal, emotional, and hedonistic. Their responses were more focused around the creation and consumption of information related to themselves and the social lives of others, rather than direct usefulness of the information or the service. We also observed that such findings were backed up by nearly 30 years of research on social exchanges (both online and in the brick and mortar world): critical to viability of the social exchanges are the ways in which individuals can project and define their identities and observe and help construct the identities of others.[17]

The research on social exchanges also suggests that one reason consumers may both use a product and share information about it with their friends is to make a statement about their own *self-identity*. An easy and obvious example is our participation in products that facilitate social networking. We join social networks to connect with friends, find old loves, find new loves, find jobs, and show off our families. Most of these involve creating and managing an online identity through posting comments, pictures, links, and so on. Identity theory refers to these actions as *exhibitionism,* because we are portraying an imagined and polished version of ourselves online. The flip side of this is consuming the content posted by others, which identity theory refers to as *voyeurism*. These two-sided concepts of *self-identity* were both hinted at within our interviews and validated later on with statistical modeling to be highly correlated with both the misbehaviors of customers (co-production) and with viral growth.

Examples of customer misbehavior with products for reasons of defining and exhibiting an identity abound in both the online and the 'real' world. For example, one might misuse used FedEx shipping containers by making furniture out of them. In so doing, the person might be trying to say that they are environmentally conscious in an attempt to avoid sending the boxes to a landfill. Or perhaps they are saying that they are a clever designer. Animal lovers may be driven to create pet pages on either Friendster or Facebook in an effort to define an identity stating the degree to which they love and care about their animals, or in order to share information about their love of pets with friends who have similar interests. Drivers of hybrid vehicles may be as concerned about the statement that they are environmentally conscious as they are about the positive impact they may have on climate change. People may wear their clothes in a unique (and from a manufacturer's perspective) unintended way so as to show off their undergarments, and in so doing affiliate with a certain culture or make a specific statement.

As self-identity helps answer the question of why a customer may misbehave, it becomes the top of our pyramid of viral growth. We aren't suggesting that usefulness, ease of use, and identity are the only reasons why products and services exhibit sustained, rapid growth – simply that they are important and also some of the most neglected reasons. More importantly, we argue that there are actions that firms can take within their product development processes to ensure that each one is addressed. Getting all three 'right' significantly increases the chances of creating a set of products that have viral growth possibilities.

THE ORGANIZATION OF THIS BOOK

In this book we seek to answer the following critical questions:

1. Why should *all* businesses care about viral growth and what are some of the key drivers of viral growth?

2. How can companies leverage these drivers to design and build products that encourage viral growth?

3. What processes and mindset changes are necessary to continue to stimulate growth over time?

Chapter 1 considers the term 'viral' and answers several questions around its meaning, usage, and value to the enterprise. The chapter explains in both prose and mathematically what the term 'viral' means in order to arm the executive and operator with a critical tool for measuring the success of their product and service endeavors. Furthermore it goes on to illustrate the difference between something that is 'viral' and that which contributes to long-term success and viability of any enterprise – 'viral growth'. The key difference between these two terms is the notion of retention of users. 'Viral' can mean any 'flash in the pan' effect (seen with YouTube videos that are passed between users and watched only once), whereas 'viral growth' considers users returning to a site or product, such as in the case of Facebook. The metrics of success that we offer are called the 'viral coefficient' and the 'viral growth equation'. Those responsible for defining and building these products will want to read the footnotes closely and ensure they understand the equation behind these equations. Leveraging the math and meaning behind going 'viral', Chapter 1 further discusses why this growth is valuable to any business. We explore 'virality' through the online media sensation, 'The Honey Badger', and the real-world business of Tupperware. These stories serve to show both how the viral coefficient is calculated and how it can serve to drive success within a business context.

Chapter 2 moves on to consider some of the features that past research has shown to be critical to technology adoption. Leveraging Davis' 1989 *MIS Quarterly* paper, we delve into the product attributes of *perceived usefulness* and *perceived ease of use* and their effects on the user acceptance and adoption of technology.[18] These concepts become the cornerstone for a practitioner-focused model that helps to explain how and why certain products 'go viral'. This in turn sets us up to answer the questions of 'what causes products to achieve viral growth?' and 'how can we build products that have a better chance of achieving viral growth?' Senior executives will want to read this chapter quickly, familiarizing themselves with the terms and resulting effects of perceived usefulness and perceived ease of use on technology adoption. Those in positions of building and defining products should read more closely in order to better grasp these concepts as they are critical to the model that we begin to build in Chapter 3.

Chapter 3 is an important chapter for everyone and is worthy of a focused read. In this chapter we discuss our key finding that many viral products achieve 'virality' in ways not originally imagined by the designers of the products being used. We incorporate this new finding with the concepts presented within Chapter 2 and build two models: the first describes a virtuous cycle of customer misbehavior that helps fuel viral growth; the second is a model that begins to describe how viral growth and viral success is achieved. We explore how internal biases very often cause companies to 'snatch defeat' from the jaws of 'viral victory'. The senior executive will both want to be mindful of how to build processes that help identify innovative user ('mis')behavior and guard against the common mistakes that keep such behavior from being valuable. Managers and individual contributors responsible for building viral products will want to become conversant and even expert in the models that we present in the chapter.

Chapters 4, 5, and 6 delve into the least known identified driver of viral growth, and a key component of our model, the concept of *self-identity*. Here we will answer the question 'why are customers motivated to participate in misbehavior?' We will explore this topic by first grasping the concept itself in Chapter 4, then going on to investigate two aspects of self-identity – self-verification and public displays of ourselves. We interleave corporate stories and research to explain how *self-identity* motivates customers to use, misuse, and share experiences of usage of the products. Why are consumers driven to share product usage with their peers? Why would users take a product like Facebook, which was clearly meant to connect humans and create accounts for their pets? What could possibly drive someone to not only create furniture out of FedEx shipping containers but show the world through YouTube videos that he was doing so?

In Chapter 5 we look at how people use self-verification to reinforce their own perception of their self-identity. Interestingly we tend to avoid people who have opinions about our self-identity that differ from our own and gravitate towards those who reinforce our belief of our self-identity.

In Chapter 6 we explore how individuals use visible cues to represent their self-identity. Individuals use luxury goods such as high-end watches, jewelry, and clothing, as well as environmentally-friendly products (such as hybrid vehicles), or even sports teams to form and display their self-identity as part of social bonding processes.

Both Chapters 5 and 6 contain material that will be interesting for both practitioners and researchers. From senior executives to product managers to engineers and designers, understanding one aspect of the motivations of our customers will help build better products and retain more customers.

The following two chapters are dedicated to showing how the model has worked for a handful of companies from our research. Chapter 7 shows how many companies 'Got it Right'. While these companies didn't have our model to use, they were successful through intuition, trial and error – and even a little bit of luck. The chapter cruises through a number of industries and shows how our model can explain the success of companies within those industries. From Facebook and Twitter, to the war in Iraq and the Fast Food industry, we apply our model and show how certain elements have helped lead to successful growth for companies.

Models are even more useful and powerful when they help explain not only how to be successful, but also what actions should be avoided to minimize the possibility for failure. It's important to note that in most cases a failure to enable user identity and participate in co-production with your users will limit the probability of achieving viral success – not doom your business to failure. Many successful businesses have been built without products that specifically speak to an individual's need to define and verify their identities. Businesses are successful every day without engaging their users in a process of *co-production*. But few, if any, of these businesses achieve viral success.

And, as Chapter 8 shows, when a company competes in an industry with viral potential against fierce competition intensely focused on growth, a failure to abide by our model may in fact mean disaster. We look at how the model led to incredible initial success for one company, Friendster, and then how a failure to follow it led to Friendster's ultimate demise within the United States. Both of these chapters contain material that will be interesting for both practitioners and researchers. By highlighting the fantastic accomplishments and incredible catastrophes of companies experiencing the propulsion of viral growth success (Chapter 7) and the explosion of viral growth failure (Chapter 8) they help bring our model to life.

We conclude in Chapter 9 with a summary of the future of service innovation and how to compete successfully within the new world order.

1
Why is Viral Growth Important?

'This is the honey badger. Watch it run in slow motion. It's pretty badass. Look, it runs all over the place. "Woah, watch out!", says that bird. Ew it's got a snake? Oh, it's chasing a jackal? Oh my gosh!' If you read this and the voice in your head sounded like a high-pitched, effeminate male, then you've undoubtedly seen the YouTube video 'The Crazy Nastyass Honey Badger (original narration by Randall)'. It was uploaded on 18 January 2011 by user 'czg123' and has been viewed over 56 million times.[1] The video features original footage of the tough and ornery Honey badgers taken from a National Geographic special that aired in 2007.

According to the *New York Observer* the 'Crazy Nastyass Honey Badger' video was the brainchild of Christopher Gordon[2] (not a guy named Randall) – an actor, writer, comedian, and 'Randall's Personal Asst.'[3] In an email interview by Michael Humphrey, Contributor at *Forbes*, we learn that Gordon's inspiration for the video came from his father's work on Marlon Perkins' 'Mutual of Omaha's Wild Kingdom' as a cameraman.[4] Between his father's film footage and his twice-weekly trips to the zoo with his grandmother, he developed the habit of narrating everything.

With memorable quotes such as 'honey badger don't give a shit' or 'honey badger don't care', the video became an instant hit. It was covered within the first 30 days by humor blogs such as 'Funny or Die' and 'Huffington Post' as well as mainstream entertainment sites like TMZ.[5] The authors of this book became aware of the video in January 2011 when Marty's friend posted the video on Facebook. He then passed it in email along to Mike and several other colleagues. Kalle (Marty and Mike's doctoral advisor at the time) stared in disbelief, believing that the foundations of education were sure to crumble beneath him, as Marty showed the video to a group of academics between meetings. Marty singlehandedly invited dozens of people to view the video, many of whom could be seen later excitedly discussing the video amongst themselves and immediately sharing it on Facebook, or emailing a link to it to friends and colleagues.

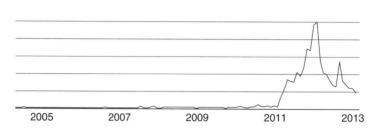

Figure 1.1 *Google Search for 'Honey Badger'*[6]

Source: Google and the Google logo are registered trademarks of Google Inc., used with permission.

While the video became a huge Internet sensation, its attraction as an entertainment destination was short lived. Figure 1.1 shows that prior to Randall's video, not many people were searching for 'honey badgers' on the web. During 2011 the interest skyrocketed, while plateauing at the end of the year. After a year in the spotlight, interest in the web search term 'honey badgers' started to wane, falling almost as quickly as it rose.

The Honey badger video teaches us several key points that we would like to present in this chapter about viral growth. First, it shows how ideas can spread from one individual to another very quickly. Marty alone was responsible for inviting dozens of people to view the video. Second, it helps us see the effect of virality without the power of retention. While the Honey badger video was wildly popular in 2011, by 2013 its popularity had disappeared. We'll cover both of these points in more detail in this chapter as well as answer the question of why viral growth is important. First we need to define the term *viral growth*.

VIRAL GROWTH CLIFF NOTES

Viral growth is achieved when the users of a product cause, on average, more than one additional user, per existing user, to use a product or service. In other words, each user of a product influences more than one additional user to begin using the product during some specified time period. If a product has five users at the end of time period 1, it will have more than ten users using the product in time period 2, more than 20 in time period 3, and so on.

An existing user of a product influencing a friend, colleague, or relative to start using a product can occur in a variety of ways. One method is very direct. A user invites a bunch of friends to start using a product by sending an email with a link to the product. In the real world the user might send a postcard that advertises the product. Another method, that is much less direct, is that people might see another individual using the product. Before a night out, a husband might notice his wife using an online product to search for restaurants. If the next time the husband needs a restaurant he starts using that product, then his spouse has influenced him into using the product. There are as many ways as you can imagine – both directly and indirectly – to influence another user to begin using a product. Of course, marketers for years have been trying to figure out new ways for this to occur.

This provides a very high-level explanation of how viral growth occurs. For a more in-depth explanation, continue reading the next section. For those who don't like math, or just really don't want to understand the details of this phenomenon, skip ahead two sections in this chapter to one entitled 'Why do we want to achieve viral growth?', where you'll get to read about two companies that achieved viral growth.

WHAT IS VIRAL GROWTH?

For our purposes, *growth* can be defined as building a user base for a product or service. If we had one user yesterday and we gain another user today we have 100 per cent growth day-over-day. The term 'viral' is an adjective that describes the picking up of an object or information that can induce agents possessing it to replicate it, resulting in a myriad of new copies being spread around. The etymology of the term *viral* dates to 1989 according to the *Oxford English Dictionary*. At that time it came to mean the 'rapid spread of information', in addition to its earlier meaning of the spreading of viruses or germs during a contagion of a disease. A *viral video* would thus be one that induces people to view it and share it with other people, resulting in a growing number of views. One interesting point about being viral is that it does not have to be a purposeful replication. In some instances, people might intentionally share a video with their friends, but in other situations people might see a celebrity watching a video and then view it themselves. The viewing of the video has been replicated, but not by active participation of the celebrity.

The presence of such a fast growth pattern that follows the spread of information in social networks has justified the use of the epidemiological term 'viral growth' to characterize these patterns. The *spread* of information and its consequent use in a population is like that of a virus spreading through a population. Though in their everyday life people do not intentionally spread viruses, they can figuratively do so in their social networks by sharing information about rumors, services, features, benefits of a site, or just by telling others about their positive use experiences.[7] Combining these two words we can form the term *viral growth* that we define as *the increase in the user base of a product or service resulting from people's action to induce other people in their networks to repeat their usage of the product or service.*

While viral growth has only reached the mainstream vernacular in the past decade when the hyper-growth Internet services made it popular, the idea of viral growth dates back to 1976, with Richard Dawkins' publication of *The Selfish Gene*. Dawkins' book analyzed evolution as a cultural phenomenon, where instead of genes controlling the evolution ideas called 'memes' would control the process. A meme is a framework for thinking about things – an idea, behavior, or style, such as wearing white after Labor Day, the phrase 'You had me at "hello"' from the 1996 film *Jerry McGuire*, or the Honey badger story. It can be anything passed from person to person where the rate of acceptance and proliferation are likely to depend on several factors such as entertainment value, news worthiness, educational value, or sheer popularity.

One significant difference between biological evolution and cultural evolution is the pace at which cultural evolution can take place. Memes can spread much faster than genes can replicate, even when compared to the very fast ten-day metamorphosis cycle of a fruit fly. In that amount of time a meme can spread around the Internet and become old news. Viral growth is achieved when a meme spreads very fast, without the conscious plan and effort to spread it. At the same time the growth in a user base will follow a power-law distribution until the adoption reaches a point of non-displacement.[8]

A power law expresses a mathematical relationship between two quantities in which the frequency that an event occurs varies as a power (or exponentiation) of some attribute of that event. In the case of the Honey badger video, the upward curve of Figure 1.1 (the viral growth phase) is a power of the previous viewings and subsequent shares. To achieve the sharp incline in growth, the cumulative viewers for any given day have to share (on average) the video more than once. Power-law distributions are also sometimes called scale-invariant or scale-free distributions, because a power law is the only distribution that is the same whatever scale we look at it on.[9]

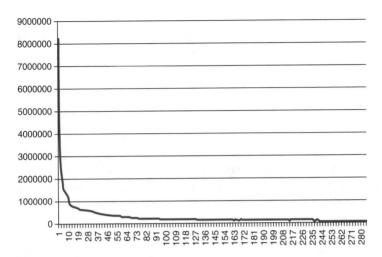

Figure 1.2 *US City Populations*

Few real-world distributions follow a power law over their entire range, especially for smaller values of the event. For example, the population of cities follows a power-law distribution above the minimum population of 40,000. In Figure 1.2 we have plotted the populations of the top 285 US cities according to the 2010 US Census. As you can see, a few cities have the majority of the population and then the amounts drop off quickly. The top city, New York with 8.2 million people, has three times as many people as just the third city, Chicago, with 2.7 million people.

Armed with this initial definition of *viral growth* and understanding of power laws, we next explore factors that define viral growth.

WHAT ARE THE COMPONENTS OF VIRAL GROWTH?

While achieving viral growth can be elusive, calculating and predicting the growth under certain conditions can be accurately determined due to well-defined structural conditions that characterize such growth. In order to do so requires acquiring and estimating information about pivotal factors that affect the spread of the information or ideas. This process of spreading is known as *contagion*, which can be defined as rapid communication of an influence. It is also derived from an epidemiological term relating to the spread of infectious disease.[10] Contagion simply deals with the rate at which infected new users become 'converted' to use a particular product or service. Factors that affect contagion, as known from epidemiological studies, include first *fan-out* and *conversion*, both of which we will discuss below. For a more complete coverage of how the term 'viral growth' was derived from the study of contagious diseases, see Appendix A.

The viral growth of a product or service is determined by the extent to which current users send requests to their friends or colleagues to participate in a service and whether those individuals 'convert' and become users as well. To describe the rate of this process, Kalyanam coined the concept of a viral index[11] or viral coefficient[12] that predicts how quickly viral growth can occur for a service provider. The viral coefficient (C_v) predicts the number of new users that will be generated by one existing user through influencing, recommending, suggesting, sharing, and so on. It is a function of the *fan-out* (number of new users invited per existing user) multiplied by the *conversion rate* (number of new users converted to using the service) and is defined as:

$$C_v = fan\text{-}out * conversion\ rate \tag{1}$$

C_v must exceed 1.0 to generate viral growth. The variable *fan-out* is the number of individuals an existing user introduces to the product or service. This factor can be influenced by a wide variety of factors including the ease with which users can share recommendations and linking existing users with potential new users through a process dubbed a 'social cascade'.[13] *Conversion rate* is the number of new users that convert to using the service or product after receiving an invitation (from the fan-out). It is affected by factors such as the perceived value, learning effort (ease of use),[14] service quality,[15] and perceived entertainment.[16]

From our Honey badger story, Marty initially was the recipient of another person's transmission (or fan-out) of the video. He subsequently converted by watching the video himself. He then invited people via email and displayed the video in public settings. A number of email users converted, and by definition all of the people in the public viewing 'converted', because they watched the video. Therefore Marty was responsible for a C_v far greater than 1.0. The sum of all shares (all people like Marty sharing the video) divided by the number of sharing people and subsequently multiplied by the resulting conversion (or views) for the month of January would be the Honey badger's C_v for January of 2011.

Although C_v measures service growth, it cannot identify a sustainable growth strategy for a product or service provider, because it fails to measure *sustained growth* – growth that takes into account a loss of users to competitors' new services, or users dropping the service because of loss of interest or value. A high C_v without the new users returning to use the service results in the 'Slashdot effect' – so named after the popular technology news site, Slashdot.org. When an article on Slashdot mentions a small site, the ensuing traffic spike can cause the small site to slow down or fail. Once the article has run the news cycle and is no longer popular, the small site's traffic returns to normal with no recurring or sustained traffic. This 'moment in the spotlight' might be thrilling, but it doesn't produce a sustained growth in new readers or users for the small site. This effect can be seen in the 'Honey badger' curve of Figure 1.1, albeit in a somewhat biased way since the graph shows all searches for the term and not just direct views of the video. Clearly a large number of people shared and subsequently watched the video, but ultimately those users did not continue to return to watch the video over and over again resulting in the downward trend.

For the growth to be truly viable, the product or service must increase its number of *cumulative users*, over a certain period. This requires new users to not only join, but to stick around. To calculate the cumulative users we must multiply the C_v by a *retention rate* and raise the product to the exponent of the *frequency* (number of times the service is used per cycle i.e. intensity of social exchanges in any social network, where the cycle is a fixed time period e.g. one day, one week, one month, which depends on the feature and nature of social exchange). The calculation of cumulative users is known as the **viral growth equation:**

$$cumulative\ users = (C_v * retention\ rate)^{(frequency)} \qquad (2)$$

Obviously the C_v of the product or service expresses the total number of cumulative users if we can estimate all the factors that influence it. First, if viral coefficients remain below 1 the exponential growth is impossible. But similarly we must retain most of the users we convert. Therefore combinations of both rates need to meet specific threshold conditions in order for exponential growth to ensue. Figure 1.3 shows several examples of how alternative combinations of values for *conversion rate* and *retention rate* affect the number of *cumulative users*.

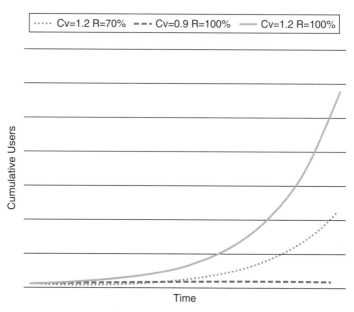

Figure 1.3 *Viral Growth Equation*

The solid line shows C_v at 1.2 (well above 1 which is needed for viral growth) and *retention rate* at 100 per cent. This is the classic 'hockey stick' growth pattern, so named because the graph resembles the shape of a hockey stick, which we typically associate with the experienced viral growth of some products or services. The dotted line shows C_v again at 1.2 but the *retention rate* at only 70 per cent, still we have a *cumulative users* growth rate that any product or service provider would love to have. To show the massive effect of C_v, the dashed line shows the C_v of 0.9 and the *retention rate* back at 100 per cent. Notice that there is no viral growth in this last example. Despite retaining 100 per cent of users this last product cannot achieve viral growth, because it is not capable of bringing in one new user for every existing user.

The equations 1 and 2 suggest a variety of ways the number of cumulative users of a product or service can be improved. Walking through the equation, when on average each user shares (fan-out) the product more than once and a majority of those users attempt to use the product (conversion) this will result in a $C_v > 1.0$. Furthermore if each of these users on average repeats the usage of the site (retention) over the course of the year (cycle) more than once (frequency) the result will repeat itself. The viral growth equation tells us that by sharing information about new services, new features or benefits of services, or just telling others, either intentionally or accidentally, growth will be inevitably achieved. It sounds so simple, right?

Accordingly product and service providers can utilize many strategies to increase the viral coefficient, most of which can be categorized under viral marketing (fan-out), or they can innovate with new features and services that increase the scope and intensity of user experience and cycle of frequency thereby affecting conversion or retention. This, in turn, requires investing in processes through which service innovation can take place quickly. Indeed, the question of how to influence factors that underlie the value of viral coefficient, conversion rate, and retention rate to ultimately achieve viral growth is the foundational question that our research began with. We are going to share our insights on this topic in the remainder of this book, but first we must address the question of why a product or service provider should attempt to achieve viral growth.

WHY DO WE WANT TO ACHIEVE VIRAL GROWTH?

Whether your business is an online social network, an auction site, an e-commerce platform, or a real-world store, all these businesses will rely on consumer traffic – either clicks and eyeballs or feet and bodies. When a product or service is 'sticky' (in our equation the frequency is high for the defined interval length or 'cycle'), the traffic translates to tangible business and growth. Think of this in terms of how many times you return to your local Target or Wal-Mart store (frequency) within a month, a quarter, or a year (cycle). Failing to achieve sufficient growth dooms a company to tepid business, poor financials, and ultimately to failure. Even if you achieve good growth, the market value of your company can tumble precipitously in a short period of time, if you cannot sustain it.

Some online businesses have achieved hyper-fast viral growth, as exemplified by Twitter's growth in 2009 at a staggering 1382 per cent.[17] Products and services that display such viral growth are those that can be adopted by and passed between users incrementally, gaining exponential momentum in adoption rates as time progresses. Viral growth should therefore be a goal for an array of businesses launching today, because it is a way for a company to achieve significant market share faster, and with the flexibility to target new markets in the midst of growth. In turn, viral growth allows companies to achieve investor returns faster, assuming the company has figured out how to monetize the traffic. Simply put, for businesses that do not operate in natural monopolies or oligopolies, viral growth will most quickly enable them to create a defensible position.

Viral Growth on the Internet – Friendster vs. Facebook

It is easy to understand and instructive to learn the importance of the principle of viral growth, if we consider the effects of the growth of social networking sites. A terrific example of the power of viral growth is the comparison of the fates of Friendster and Facebook. Both launched at almost the same time, were equally well funded, and both hired talented teams, but one ultimately achieved sustainable viral growth while the other did not. Consequently their fortunes differed markedly.

Friendster was founded by Jonathan Abrams and Chris Emmanuel in 2002 in Mountain View, California, before the creation, launch, and adoption of Myspace, Facebook, LinkedIn, and other social networking sites. Friendster's purpose was to establish a safer, more effective way to meet new people by browsing user profiles and connecting to friends, and friends of friends.[18] This allowed members to expand their network more rapidly than in real life.

Friendster.com went live in March 2003 and was adopted by three million users within the first few months. As its popularity increased, page load times slowed – users waited longer for each attempt to use the site. At one point, a Friendster web page took as long as 40 seconds to download. The main reason for this was that Friendster had a product feature, known as the friend-graph (or F-graph), that caused the site's poor performance. The F-graph calculated the four degrees of connection for every user, every time a new connection between people was made. Technical difficulties in solving this computational problem proved too pedestrian for the Board of Directors to address and thus they were left to the engineers to resolve.

Over the next three years the Board named four CEOs, some of them remaining in office for only a few months. During the five-year term of Kent Lindstrom, one of the earliest investors in Friendster, a new team was recruited, technical challenges were solved, and the company prioritized the Asian market. This resulted in Friendster becoming the leading social network in some Asian countries, and it received $30 million in additional funding from Kleiner Perkins and Benchmark Capital.

In 2008, Friendster hired ex-Google executive Richard Kimber as the CEO and had a membership base of more than 115 million registered users. On 9 December 2009, it was finally acquired by MOL, a Malaysian company, for $26.4 million despite receiving funding in October 2003 at a reported valuation of $53 million.

The story of Friendster seems like a relative success until we compare it to the meteoric rise of Facebook. Mark Zuckerberg founded Facebook with his college roommates and fellow computer science students, Eduardo Saverin, Dustin Moskovitz, and Chris Hughes, while they were students at Harvard University. The website's membership was initially limited to Harvard students as a version of hotornot.com, but was expanded to other colleges, then to high school students, and finally to anyone over the age of 13. The site was ranked as the most used social network worldwide by monthly active users in 2009, and had over 500 million active members by 2010. In 2008 the fastest growing demographic was 25 years old and older, while in 2009 the fastest growing demographic was 35–54 year olds.[19]

In terms of usage – a key component in the viral growth equation – Facebook has over 900 million total users with 35 million users updating their status each day, uploading 2.5 billion photos each month, and sharing 3.5 billion pieces of content each week. The average user has 100 friends and 2.6 billion minutes are spent on the site each day.[20] Facebook, having achieved exponential user growth, announced revenues of over $1 billion in 2011, going public in the summer of 2012, which raised $16 billion of capital and valued the company at over $104 billion.

As noted, Friendster and Facebook were launched at almost the same time, had equally talented teams, and were both well-funded; yet one achieved sustained viral growth while the other did not. The resulting valuation for investors was $26.4 million for one and $104 billion for the other. This teaches us that with social networking, and anything on the web, failing to achieve viral growth dooms a company to failure. Even if one achieves good growth for some time, the market value of the company can tumble precipitously in a short period of time if one cannot sustain it.

Real-World Viral Growth – Tupperware

It's relatively easy to see how viral growth needs to be, and can be, achieved with online services such as Twitter and Facebook, where users are engaged in producing content such as 140-character pithy comments or pictures of their latest vacation, but what about the world of atoms – the physical products and services? Most of us are familiar with Tupperware, plastic containers used in our houses to store or serve food and various other items. What you might not know is that the Tupperware story is an example of non-Internet viral growth.[21]

Earl Tupper developed Tupperware in 1946 and patented the 'burping seal' for which the brand was known. However we can argue that not many of us would know the brand, if it wasn't for the efforts of Brownie Wise, the former sales representative for Stanley Home Products, who developed the direct marketing strategy that made Tupperware a household name. The marketing strategy, also known as the 'home party plan', empowered women in the early 1950s who refused to 'go back to the kitchen' after World War II, and instead insisted on having a place in the workforce.[22] These party plans were where women invited friends and neighbors to a combined social event/ sales presentation. This word-of-mouth model of direct sales relied upon trusted relationships primarily between women and proved incredibly successful. While many of us growing up in the 1960s and 1970s remember comedians joking about Tupperware parties, the result was just more free publicity. In 1958, Mr. Tupper sold the company for $16 million to Rexall Drug Co., renounced his US citizenship, and ended up living in Costa Rica until he died in 1983 at the age of 76. Unfortunately before the sale, Mr. Tupper ousted Ms. Wise from the company, believing that suitors of the company would have no interest in a female executive (according to Laurie Kahn, who wrote, produced, and directed the 2004 PBS documentary 'Tupperware!'). The company spun back off as an independent company on 31 May 1996 and continues to thrive, relying primarily on the party plan. A few years ago, Rick Goings, the Chairman and CEO, boasted that a Tupperware party was held somewhere in the world every 2.3 seconds, but with a direct sales force of over 2.6 million, that rate is closer to a party every 1.7 seconds.[23] In Figure 1.4, Tupperware's performance is compared with a competitor, Rubbermaid, showing Tupperware up over 60 per cent, while Rubbermaid is down nearly 20 per cent over the 17-year period since the spinout.

Hopefully, by this point you, along with every other 18-year-old would-be-entrepreneur, are convinced on the value of viral growth. However you've probably realized from these stories that viral growth is somewhat akin to catching lighting in a bottle. It is a rare event,

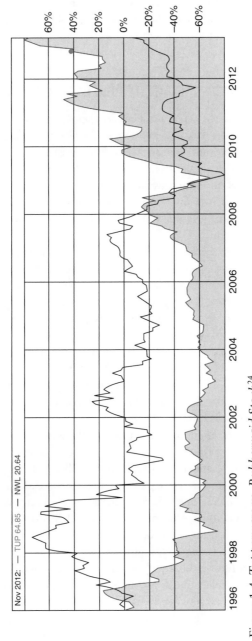

Figure 1.4 *Tupperware vs. Rubbermaid Stock*[24]

Source: © 2013 Yahoo! Inc.

made more likely by the advent of the Internet or some specific social condition (such as suburbia housewives and their need for socializing), but still exceptional. So, where does that leave us? Should we give up or push on in the quest for viral growth?

WHAT IF YOU CAN'T ACHIEVE VIRAL GROWTH?

While true viral growth, where the viral coefficient (C_v) is greater than 1, might be rare, there is still a lot we can achieve with viral replication of our products and services. We are going to refer to this type of organic – with a viral coefficient less than 1 but that is achieved by word-of-mouth – as sub-viral growth or organic growth. By using other means of growth such as marketing, advertising, and search engine optimization,[25] we can leverage this sub-viral growth to amplify these into significant growth.[26]

Let's look at how we can use organic growth to amplify paid-for growth, such as from advertisements. If we have a site to which we want to attract users, we can leverage non-organic growth by purchasing advertisements. We can then leverage our organic growth to augment the paid-for growth, resulting in higher growth rates. As an example, in Figure 1.5 we have plotted the monthly growth of users on our own site. The solid line is 100,000 new users per month, assuming a loss of 2 per cent of users each month. While the growth is impressive, we can do better. If we amplify our growth by including organic growth, with a viral coefficient of 0.70, we achieve three times the total users, plotted as a dashed line.

This idea of using organic, sub-viral growth to amplify more traditional marketing is finding roots in quantitative research. Sharad Goel, Duncan Watts, and Daniel Goldstein – all three from Yahoo! Research – recently presented a paper at the 13th ACM Conference on Electronic Commerce that described the diffusion patterns of seven online services, including Yahoo! Voice, Friend Sense (a Facebook application), news stories sent via Twitter, and a psychological test called 'The Secretary Game'.[27] Despite the fact that each of these had very different profiles of how users shared, the vast majority of the sharing cascades were small, terminating within one degree of the initial 'seed'. Adoption or viewing by users from a chain of referrals was extremely rare. But the good news, according to Goel et al, is that while most new services don't go viral like the flu, they can get a 20 or

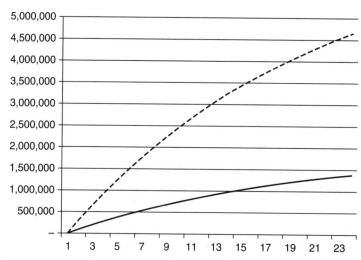

Figure 1.5 *Amplification Growth – http://afkpartners.com*

30 per cent boost in return, where for every ten adoptees of a conventional marketing effort, another two or three people will adopt something organically.[28]

CONCLUSION

We started this chapter by defining the term 'viral growth' as *the increase in the user base of a product or service, resulting from people's action to induce other people in their networks to repeat their usage of the product or service.*

We learned the etymology of the concept and term. We also learned that viral growth with a viral coefficient greater than 1 follows a power-law distribution. We calculated the viral coefficient by multiplying *fan-out* (number of new users invited per existing user) by the *conversion rate* (number of new users converted to using the service). As it turns out however high viral coefficients aren't enough. What we really need is viral growth with a high number of cumulative users. What is known as the **viral growth equation** can then be calculated by multiplying the viral coefficient by a *retention rate* (how many users continue using the product or service) and raising the product to the exponent of the *frequency* (number of times the service is used per cycle i.e. intensity of social exchanges) and *length of the cycle* (that is, a fixed time period, such as one day, one week, one month, which depends on the feature and nature of social exchange).

Armed with this understanding of viral growth we next explored the question of why one would want to achieve viral growth. We examined two scenarios to answer this question. The first scenario compared Facebook and Friendster, two Internet-based social networks that started within months of each other, had seemingly similar opportunities, and yet achieved dramatically different results. The second scenario investigated Tupperware, a classic example of viral growth in the pre-Internet era, that achieved remarkable results for many individuals who were involved with the company over the past six decades.

Finally we explored the idea of how we might leverage existing users to influence new users, even if we can't achieve true viral growth. We found that even with a viral coefficient less than 1, we can achieve substantial growth amplification by following ideas of viral growth, and informed by the viral equation. One example demonstrated a total growth rate three times greater, with a viral coefficient of 0.70, than without this user-influenced growth. The conclusion drawn from these examples is that any amount of user-based viral growth is a good thing. While it works extraordinarily well for Internet-based products and services, the concept can be applied to any real-world commerce as well.

Next we need to explore the factors that influence the viral coefficient and retention rate. Through our research we discovered that how companies respond to customers' misusing of their product could affect the factors of viral growth. We also uncovered that an underlying motivation of customers to use, and possibly misuse, products and services is the creation and management of their self-identity. These and other factors will be covered in the next few chapters.

Summary

- Viral growth can be defined as *the increase in the user base of a product or service, achieved by people inducing other people to repeat the usage.*

- The viral growth equation is:

$$cumulative\ users = (viral\ coefficient * retention\ rate)^{(frequency)}$$

- Viral growth, when achieved, can create enormous value for companies, with skyrocketing sales and usage of products or services.

- True viral growth, where the viral coefficient is greater than 1, is very rare but any amount of growth that comes from people influencing other people can augment more traditional marketing methods.

2
Technological Factors

In the summer of 1941, a young graduate student from urban Milwaukee, Wisconsin, named Neal C. Gross, found himself in the rural countryside 50 miles west of Ames, Iowa. Told that farmers began work early in the morning, he got up early enough to ensure that he was standing on the doorstep of the first farmhouse before sunrise. While not familiar with farming, he was familiar with hard work. Gross conducted 21 interviews that first day, averaging 14 per day for the length of the study, accumulating overall a total of 345 personal interviews of Iowa farmers. Showing his ignorance of agrarian subjects, when asked by one farmer how he suggested controlling the noxious weed *horse nettles*, Gross responded that the farmer should call a veterinarian to look at the sick horse.[1]

It is in this rural Iowa countryside more than 70 years ago that our journey begins into revealing how technological factors influence the viral growth of products and services. We will start by discussing how innovations progress through society as they glide through the innovation diffusion curve. We will then progress to discussing the lifecycle of technology adoption. We end this chapter with a discussion of the technology adoption model that helps describe some of the primary drivers of both the adoption lifecycle and the innovation diffusion curve. Interestingly the early research on understanding how innovations are adopted happened not within the hallowed halls of a research institution but rather the rural confines of an agriculturally-focused school. Sit back, pull on your work boots, and let's return to our story.

DIFFUSION OF INNOVATIONS

One of Gross' faculty advisors, Bryce Ryan, had only arrived at Iowa State University three years earlier and was intrigued by the question of noneconomic influences on economic behavior. This topic had become important to him during his doctoral studies in the Department of Sociology at Harvard University. Since Iowa State University was an agricultural college, Ryan decided to investigate the diffusion of hybrid seed corn with funding provided by the Iowa Agricultural Experiment Station (IAES). The IAES was a research and development organization within Iowa State University that had played an important role in developing hybrid seeds, and thus had a vested interest in understanding the factors that influenced farmers' adoption of hybrid seeds. These hybrid seeds also had a potentially important impact for farmers as they could lead to increased corn yields of about 20 per cent per acre. Ryan roped Gross into the study by offering him the use of the data for his master's thesis, if he would personally interview the farmers in two Iowa communities.[2]

The paper that Ryan and Gross eventually published from the results of this study revealed some surprising insights. One such insight was that hybrid corn required 12 years to reach widespread diffusion or near complete saturation of potential adopters. Another insight was that the average farmer needed seven years to progress from initial awareness of the hybrid corn to full-scale adoption of the innovation, that is, planting all of the corn on his farm from hybrid seed.[3] This was the first qualitative study to demonstrate just how difficult it was for individuals to adopt new innovations. The challenges with the adoption of hybrid seeds included not only the price, which was non-trivial to Iowa farmers during the years following the Great Depression, but also a change in their habits where previously they would visually select open-pollinated seeds for planting the next season.

One criticism of the study was that the questions focused on the individual farmer rather than attempting to measure the impact of farmers' interpersonal networks. The farmer-respondents were asked where they had first learned about hybrid seeds versus who had convinced them to adopt them. Commercial seed dealers and salespeople were often mentioned as most important sources of information and were therefore most important in creating awareness of the innovation. Farmers themselves, on the other hand, were the primary drivers of adoption (typically friends and/or neighbors). Ryan and Gross' study established the importance of social networks in diffusion, but failed to investigate them completely.[4] As we have seen in many follow-up studies since this one, mass media or specialists often create awareness of an innovation, but the interpersonal communication with peers is required in order to persuade most individuals to adopt the innovation.[5]

The influence of this study on innovation diffusion for over seven decades cannot be understated. We still see their influence in today's adoption models. Three primary elements that this study contributed to the understanding of the diffusion of innovations were:

1. The variable of innovativeness was introduced, defined as the degree to which an individual is relatively earlier to adopt than are others. We'll talk more about this variable soon.

2. The cumulative number of adopters when plotted over time results in a distribution in the form of an S-shaped curve (see Figure 2.1). When the number of adopters over time is plotted on a frequency basis, a normal or bell-shaped curve is formed (see Figure 2.2).

3. The sources of information about the innovation were different at various stages in the decision-making process, with the mass media more important at the awareness stage, and peers more important at the persuasion stage.

The story of hybrid corn seed adoption was a personal one for a young boy named Everett Rogers, growing up in the 1930s on Pinehurst Farm. His family-owned farm was located outside of the city of Carroll, Iowa, that boasted a population of 4691 in the 1930 census.[6] Rogers' father loved electromechanical innovations, such as bigger

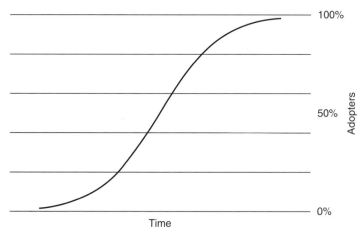

Figure 2.1 *S-Curve*

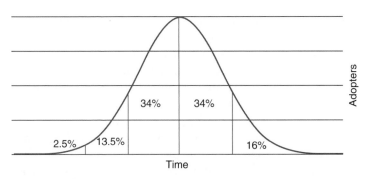

Figure 2.2 *Bell Curve*

tractors with rubber wheels, but was leery of biological–chemical innovations such as hybrid seeds, despite their proclaimed benefits of greater yield and drought resistance. In 1936 a severe drought hit Iowa and the corn on the Pinehurst Farm wilted under the sweltering sun. In the fields belonging to the Rogers' neighbors, who had switched to hybrid seed, the corn stood tall and healthy. Young Everett Rogers' father was finally convinced to adopt hybrid seed.[7]

Growing up on a farm outside such a small town in rural Iowa, Rogers had no plans to attend university. All that changed when a high school teacher drove him and some classmates into Ames to visit Iowa State University. It was during this visit that Rogers decided to pursue a degree in agriculture. After a two-year stint serving in the Korean War, Rogers returned to Iowa State University to earn a Ph.D. in sociology and statistics in 1957. It was during his doctoral work that Rogers partnered with George Beal and Joe Bohlen to develop the Technology Adoption Lifecycle model. Their research to derive this model was based on the work done 20 years earlier by Gross and Ryan.

TECHNOLOGY ADOPTION LIFECYCLE

Rogers, Beal, and Bohlen introduced this new model, the Technology Adoption Lifecycle, in their 1957 paper, 'Validity of the concept of stages in the adoption process', published in the journal *Rural Sociology*.[8] The Technology Adoption Lifecycle model describes the adoption of new products or technological innovations based on characteristics of adopter groups related to their demographic and psychological traits. As Ryan and Gross established, the process of adoption over time is typically illustrated as a classical normal distribution or 'bell curve'. The Technology Adoption Lifecycle model divides the area under the curve into five groups, each with a distinct label (Figure 2.3). The first group is called 'innovators' for these are individuals who are willing to take risk and adopt innovations sooner than anyone else. Next is the 'early adopters' followed by the 'early majority', the 'late majority', and finally, the last group to adopt an innovation is called 'laggards'.

In a special report sponsored by the Farm Foundation, Beal and Bohlen assembled data gathered by the Subcommittee for the Study of Diffusion of New Ideas and Farm Practices of the North Central Rural Sociology Committee. In this report the psychographic profiles of the farmers adopting hybrid seed were stipulated for each adoption group.[9]

- Innovators – Larger farms, high status, active in the community

- Early Adopters – Younger, higher educated, read more papers and magazines

- Early Majority – Slightly above average in age, education, and farming experience; attend more agricultural meetings

- Late Majority – Older, less educated, and less socially active

- Laggards (Non-adopters in the report) – Least educated, oldest, receive and read the fewest bulletins, papers, and magazines

Rogers then went on to generalize the use of this model in his 1962 book, *Diffusion of Innovations*, describing how new ideas, as well as

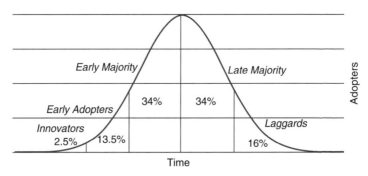

Figure 2.3 *Technology Adoption Lifecycle Groups*

technological innovations, spread through cultures. Rogers' book received worldwide acclaim and continues to this day to be printed in its fifth edition, having sold over 30,000 copies in each edition thus far. In his book, Rogers puts forth a theory to explain the conditions that must be met in order for an innovation to reach the critical tipping point that allows it to self-sustain. To start with, each individual faces their own innovation-decision that follows a five-step process:

1. Knowledge – Individual becomes aware of an innovation and has some idea of how it functions

2. Persuasion – Individual forms a favorable or unfavorable attitude toward the innovation

3. Decision – Individual engages in activities that lead to a choice to adopt or reject the innovation

4. Implementation – Individual puts the innovation to use

5. Confirmation – Individual evaluates the results of an innovation-decision already made

The innovation-decision is made through a cost–benefit analysis where the major hurdle is uncertainty. Individuals will likely adopt an innovation if they believe that it will yield some relative advantage to that which it supersedes, once all the costs are taken into consideration. These costs include monetary amounts as well as 'difficult to quantify' notions such as the amount of uncertainty and the degree to which the innovation would disrupt their daily life. Thus the newness and unfamiliarity of an innovation heavily influence the adoption decision. Because of the risk-averse nature of most individuals, the greater the uncertainty the more likely they will postpone the decision until more information is obtained. Fortunately for innovators, not everyone is like this. There is a small pocket of individuals who are highly risk-tolerant – the 'innovators' – and who just want to try out new things and poke around with them.

In the past most researchers assumed that mass media had direct, immediate, and powerful effects on individual consumers. In contrast to this, the diffusion of innovations theory pronounces that it is opinion leaders, and not mass media, who directly affect the tipping of an innovation. The diffusion process itself relies on four main influences: the innovation, communication channels, time, and a social system. This process relies heavily on human and social capital within the affected social system.

Social systems can be characterized as heterophilous or homophilous. Heterophily, *love of the different*, describes social systems that tend to encourage change from system norms. In heterophilous systems, there is more interaction between people from different backgrounds. This diversity in backgrounds and views results in greater opinion leadership and significantly higher levels of innovation. Research shows that organizations consisting of this type of diversity in experience and views tend to be more successful and more highly innovative.

Homophily, *love of the same*, describes social networks wherein individuals tend to associate and bond with others similar to themselves. People and ideas that differ from the norm are seen as strange and undesirable. With little divergence in experience and worldviews, these social systems tend towards lower levels of innovation. Within heterophilous systems, change-agents can concentrate on targeting the innovative opinion leaders and the innovation will trickle-down within the social system. Within homophilous systems however the diffusion of an innovation is far more difficult, requiring change-agents to approach a much wider group of opinion leaders. As expected, the diffusion of innovations manifests itself in different ways in various cultures and is highly subjective to the type of adopters and innovation-decision process.

The Technology Adoption Lifecycle model has been incredibly influential to researchers and practitioners over the past 50 years. Rogers' book, *Diffusion of Innovations*, alone has been cited over 48,000 times by other research papers, according to Google Scholar. The count of first, second, and even third order derivative research studies and published papers from the hundreds of papers that Rogers, Beal, and Bohlen published are innumerous. For practitioners the impact has been similar. It would be the rare business, management, or information systems college student who hasn't at least been introduced to, if not become well versed in, the groupings of innovators, early adopters, early majority, late majority, and laggards. Popular practitioner authors have also used the Technology Adoption Lifecycle as a jumping off point for their theories. In his book *Crossing the Chasm*,[10] Geoffrey Moore proposes a variation of this original Technology Adoption Lifecycle by suggesting that for disruptive innovations there is a gap or *chasm* between the first two adopter groups (innovators/early adopters) and the early majority.

In order to continue our journey towards understanding factors that influence viral growth, we're going to next drill down and approach the phenomenon of adoption by investigating the questions raised by Rogers' model in more detail. These include what type of knowledge first influences people to become aware of an innovation and then persuades them to adopt it. This leads us to probe how individuals build up intentions to do something – like adopting corn seeds – and what influences this process.

TECHNOLOGY ACCEPTANCE MODEL

In the mid-1970s, two social psychology professors at University of Illinois at Urbana-Champaign, Martin Fishbein and Icek Ajzen, were frustrated with traditional attitude–behavior theories. These theories generally found weak correlations between attitudes and voluntary behaviors.[11] Together Fishbein and Ajzen proposed the Theory of Reasoned Action, which stated that a person's attitude when combined with subjective norms creates a behavioral intent. In other words, a person's *voluntary behavior* is predicted by their *attitude* toward that behavior and how he or she *thinks* other people would view them, if they carried out that behavior.

Almost two decades later, Fred Davis proposed the Technology Acceptance Model (in his doctoral thesis at the MIT Sloan School of Management) that relied on Fishbein and Ajzen's theory of reasoned action. Introduced formally in 1989 by Davis in his *MIS Quarterly* paper 'Perceived Usefulness, Perceived Ease of Use, and User Acceptance of Information Technology',[12] the Technology Acceptance Model replaces many of the attitude measures used in the Theory of Reasoned Action with the two principal technology acceptance measures – *perceived ease of use* and *perceived usefulness*. These two types of knowledge about the technology can be seen to establish fundamental blocks of knowledge in Rogers' model to initiate the adoption cycle. The Technology Acceptance Model was originally developed to 'provide an explanation of the determinants of computer acceptance that is general, capable of explaining user behavior across a broad range of end-user computing technologies and user populations, while at the same time being both parsimonious and theoretically justified'.[13] The model views factors of perceived ease of use and perceived usefulness as 'technological' enablers for encouraging adoption by users.

The model has since then been well-vetted in academic and practitioner research.

According to the Technology Acceptance Model, as depicted in Figure 2.4, perceived ease of use and perceived usefulness directly affect the individual's attitude towards using the particular piece of technology.[14] The original study of these was directed at single-user information technologies found in work environments, such as spreadsheets or order entry systems. In the intervening years many studies have extended these factors, demonstrating their applicability to consumer technology.

The logic of the model is relatively simple. People tend to use or not use a technology to the extent that they believe it will help them perform a job or task better. This belief in a product's or service's ability to help with a task is referred to in the Technology Acceptance Model as the perceived usefulness. Davis originally defined this construct, as 'the degree to which a person believes that using a particular system would enhance his or her job performance'.[15] This notion of the perceived usefulness of a system having an impact on its utilization was earlier suggested by the work of Randall Schultz and Dennis Slevin. In their 1973 paper, they revealed that the *performance dimension* of a decision model, defined as the perceived 'effect of the model on the manager's job performance', was the most highly correlated with self-prediction of use.[16]

As individuals we are all limited by our time and effort in what we are able to accomplish. The Technology Acceptance Model therefore puts forward that, with all else being equal, an application or system that is perceived to be easier to use than another is more likely to be accepted by users. Davis describes perceived ease of use as 'the degree to which a person believes that using a particular system would be free of effort'.[17] Take note that in the Technology Acceptance Model, perceived ease of use is not only a predictor of an individual's attitudes

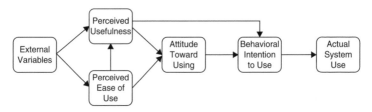

Figure 2.4 *Technology Acceptance Model*

towards usage, but it is often viewed as an antecedent of perceived usefulness. If an application is perceived to be easy to use, it is more likely to be perceived to be more useful as well. The rationale is that the easier a system is to interact with, the less effort needed to operate it, and therefore the more time and effort an individual can allocate to other activities to increase job performance.

Interestingly, as generalizable theories tend to do, the Technology Adoption Lifecycle and the Technology Acceptance Model have similar constructs and complement each other – despite originating from very different backgrounds. As you will recall, the Technology Adoption Lifecycle was derived from the diffusion of innovation work done in the 1940s to explain the adoption of hybrid corn seeds by Iowa farmers. The Technology Acceptance Model owes its origin to the social psychology work done in the 1970s to better explain the relationship between attitudes and behaviors in action in general. However, as several researchers have indicated, the constructs employed in the Technology Acceptance Model are fundamentally a subset of perceived innovation characteristics, and thus the integration of the two theories have produced highly significant results in predicting adoption.[18]

Despite the wide use of the Technology Acceptance Model, cited by over 15,000 other scholarly articles according to Google Scholar, it has received a good deal of criticism as well. This has led to several revisions of the theory while all continue to include the constructs of perceived ease of use and perceived usefulness as predictors of adoption. Criticisms of the theory include questionable heuristic value and limited predictive power,[19] despite studies finding between 40 per cent and 53 per cent of the variance in behavioral intention explained by the model,[20] and the authors' own research finding between 42 per cent and 56 per cent of the variance explained. Another criticism cited by Davis and Bagozzi themselves is that the Technology Acceptance Model assumes when someone forms an intention to act, that they will be free to act without limitation. Indeed several studies have found that intention predicts only about a third of actual use. One reason for this is that in the real world there are multiple constraints that limit an individual's freedom to act, such as the required use of the technology as part of their job, habit of using other technologies, and so on.[21]

A criticism of the Technology Acceptance Model that is of particular interest to us is the lack of a focus on the social aspects and meaning of technology usage. The model focuses solely on individual users of a single technology and essentially ignores social processes of technology development and implementation.[22] Because our initial research was centered on social networking sites, such as Facebook, Myspace, Twitter, and LinkedIn, we hypothesized that there must be a construct or factor that would take into account the social aspects of whether to adopt a particular technology or not. In Chapter 3 we will explain how these factors of perceived ease of use and perceived usefulness were integrated into our model and what other factors we added to further explain the phenomenon of viral growth.

CONCLUSION

The Technology Adoption Lifecycle introduced the terminology of 'innovators', 'early adopters', 'early majority', 'late majority', and 'laggards', as categories of people based on how relatively quickly they adopt new technologies. This adoption theory was developed from the diffusion of innovation work done in the 1940s to explain the adoption of hybrid corn seeds by Iowa farmers. Rogers, in his 1962 book, *Diffusion of Innovations,* describes how the innovation-decision is made through a cost–benefit analysis where the major hurdle is uncertainty. Individuals are more likely to adopt an innovation if they believe that it will yield some relative advantage. This decision takes into account not only the benefits, such as accomplishing some task faster, but also the costs, such as how long it will take to learn the new technology.

The Technology Acceptance Model addresses the problem of what sort of knowledge influences why people adopt certain technologies but not others. Researchers in the 1970s were trying to better explain the relationship between attitudes and behaviors when they introduced the Theory of Reasoned Action. From this was derived the Technology Acceptance Model, which introduced the constructs of *perceived ease of use* and *perceived usefulness*. While there have been numerous criticisms of the Technology Acceptance Model, it has been widely adopted for decades and has strong predictive power. As we will describe in Chapter 3, our model makes use of these constructs, but also augments them with additional constructs to make them more relevant and a better fit to explain the viral growth phenomenon.

Summary

- The Technology Adoption Lifecycle introduced the categories of 'innovators', 'early adopters', 'early majority', 'late majority', and 'laggards' to describe how relatively quickly individuals adopt new technologies.

- Rogers' book, *Diffusion of Innovations*, describes how the innovation-decision is made based on a cost–benefit analysis.

- The Technology Acceptance Model, introduced by Fred Davis and Richard Bagozzi, was derived from the Theory of Reasoned Action, which was attempting to better explain attitudes and behaviors.

- The Technology Acceptance Model makes use of constructs of *perceived ease of use* and *perceived usefulness* to explain individual's attitudes towards using new technology.

3
The Viral Model

THE iWATCHZ STORY – A VIRTUOUS CYCLE OF CO-PRODUCTION

'So now, let's look at the iPod Nano', said Steve Jobs on 1 September 2010, at a media event in San Francisco. Steve, who had eschewed his typical black mock-turtleneck for a black crewneck sweater, had his sleeves rolled up as he walked the audience through a multimedia presentation describing the first five generations of the iPod Nano. With the fifth generation iPod Nano displayed on a screen behind him, Jobs said, 'We'd like to make it smaller and we'd like to make it better'. Jobs continued to describe the changes, including the elimination of the 'click wheel' (the interface allowing iPod users to scroll through songs, change music, control volume, and so on) in favor of a multi-touch display and the addition of a clip on the back of the iPod so that it was 'instantly wearable'. At roughly 1.5 by 1.5 inches, the new iPod was 46 per cent smaller and 42 per cent lighter than its predecessor. 'No more armbands when you want to use it for athletics', declared Steve. Joking with the audience, and displaying a number of screenshots of iPod applications (including an FM radio behind him), Steve said 'It's got a clock ... One of our Board of Director members is going to clip it onto an armband as a watch'. The audience chuckled at Steve's mention of the iPod as a watch.

It's not clear if the founders of the company that ultimately became Kubxlab also chuckled at Steve's little joke. What is clear is that they would immediately embark on an incredible example of user-driven innovation extension. Just weeks after Steve's introduction of the sixth generation iPod Nano, in a dimly-lit office, far removed from the Silicon Valley, on the outskirts of Toronto, the company then known as iWatchz set up shop to create the 'first iPod Nano watch band'.[1] The first bands, known as the Q collection, had a patented clip system that allowed users to affix their new Nanos to a band that came in a variety of colors. Within one year of launch, the iWatchz bands were a top-selling accessory within the Apple.com online store and were featured at retail Apple Stores, Target, and BestBuy.

If the iWatchz story stopped there, it would be a remarkable example of customers (the engineers at Kubxlab) extending the Nano's product versatility. As with any company that identifies a customer or partner attempting to extend the usefulness of a product (or 'misbehaving'), Apple faced a series of choices. Steve's joking approach to the notion of the iPod as a watch seems to indicate that someone (ostensibly an Apple Director) had identified the potential utility of the Nano as a watch. But the lack of a watchband developed by Apple itself, coupled with Steve's joke, seems to be an indication that Apple didn't take the viability of such an accessory seriously. It's also important to understand Steve's near maniacal focus on control of both form and function for Apple's products. This is a man who, when asked to sign a Macintosh keyboard that had been produced after his departure from Apple, agreed to do so under the condition that he be allowed to remove all the 'unnecessary' keys that his successors had 'foolishly added'.[2] Considering this, it isn't outside the realm of possibility that Steve and Apple would block iWatchz and other companies from producing arm bands in favor of either no watchbands or ones created by Apple itself with Apple's take on an appropriate aesthetic design for the watchbands.

But Apple did something unusual, if not for them, then for most of the companies we researched or with which we interacted. They at first embraced their new found partners by adding them to the official Apple online store and including them within their tightly controlled real-world Apple Retail store experience. And as if this wasn't already enough, they did something even more unusual. On 4 October 2011, Apple released a firmware update (revision 1.2) for the iPod, that added 16 new stylish clock faces, including analog and digital clocks as well as a Mickey Mouse watch face.[3] In so doing, Apple went beyond a passive allowance of the misbehavior to embracing the behavior as valuable innovation as seen by its inclusion in its stores. Apple extended the usefulness of the innovation by supporting it with additional clock faces for people who might wear the Nano as a watch.

On Wednesday, 12 September 2012, Apple released the seventh generation of the Nano, moving away from the 1.5 inch square design to adopt a larger touchscreen display. Apple's stated intent was to increase the screen size of the Nano such that it could, among other things, again become a video platform.[4] As such, unlike many of the companies within our research, Apple wasn't trying to kill the misbehavior but rather was trying to improve the overall usefulness of the product. iWatchz changed their name to Kubxlab and while they still sell watchbands for the existing sixth generation Nanos, they have since moved on to providing accessories for other Apple-related products.

Interestingly, Apple has reportedly been working on a 'smart watch' that would perform 'some functions of a smart phone'.[5] Speculation from various sources seems to agree that the watch will have music, fitness, and timekeeping abilities similar to those of the iPod Nano, while adding the ability to make phone calls and connect to Bluetooth devices. What started as customer misbehavior has turned into a fully-fledged product line.

THE VIRTUOUS CYCLE OF IDENTIFYING AND ENABLING CUSTOMER MISBEHAVIOR

We've now seen a handful of stories of an interesting phenomenon that started us on our research journey. In each case, users of a product identified a novel new use for the product – one for which it was not originally intended. In each case the company that produced the product both accepted the new usage (rather than shutting it down) and equally as important *enabled* that usage. Each company dealt with some level of uncertainty in both allowing and enabling the new product usage; how large could the high-end collectible car market be for eBay and how many people would really want to wear a device intended to play songs on their wrist?

In each case, the new and unintended use also meant that the product, if successful, would potentially address some new portion of the market. In the eBay Motors case, it was the extension of the product from focusing on lower average sale price collectibles such as Beanie Babies to high average sale price collectibles such as automobiles. In the Apple and iWatchz case, it was the expansion of purchase consideration from those people interested in a lightweight portable music player to those who would also like the device to perform the functions of a watch. This new, previously unaddressed portion of the market represents an opportunity for growth. In some cases this opportunity for growth can be significant. Recall that the used car resale market in the late 1990s was $350 billion. If eBay could address only 50 basis points

(0.5 per cent) of this market, it would mean as much as $1.75 billion in gross merchandise sales, or over double the gross merchandise sales for the entire year of 1998 across all other product categories ($745 million).

It's valuable, we think, to ponder this scenario briefly as it has profound economic benefit to the enterprise. Consider first the cost of this innovation to the firm. Here we have potentially a small army of entrepreneurs, innovating on the company's behalf, at little or no cost. The gentleman who attempted to sell the Ferrari on eBay wasn't being paid by eBay to experiment with its product. Until the Ferrari was listed, no eBay employee was drawing a salary to specifically consider the opportunity in the automobile space. Nor did eBay face some great opportunity cost (initially) for investigating the feasibility of auto sales on its site as compared to working on other initiatives directed by the company. The cost of this particular customer misbehavior to the firm was minimal.

Now consider the breadth and scope of impact for the firm's products. Here we have a low- to no-cost way of testing and extending our product. The cost, if any, is just our lack of perceived control in directing how that product may get used. Aren't we best off getting more people to attempt to test and extend our product and service offerings on our behalf? Don't our shareholders want us to find low- and no-cost ways to increase our addressable market share? Don't we all want an army of innovative-minded people working for free to make us successful and increase stakeholder value? The answer, we think, to all of these questions is a very loud 'Yes!'

Research into social capital and social networks indicates that individuals who have a broad and non-overlapping network of connections are much more likely to identify creative innovations.[6] People who have a diverse array of connections within their network see a large number of ideas from their connections. This is especially true when a majority of the connections do not in turn have connections to each other (that is, that the person with the diverse connections is the only hub connecting the remainder of the connections). The person standing in the center of these non-overlapping connections acts as a 'broker',[7] passing ideas between clusters of individuals for the purposes of vetting them, and so on. This, in essence, is what is happening when companies actively look for and enable customer misbehavior and innovation. The company product or service becomes an innovation brokerage, connecting disparate groups of people. The company sits at the hub of this exchange, monitoring for unique customer misbehavior, attempting to analyze its innovation value, and enabling those activities that create the greatest opportunity for growth.

Our research indicates that the companies that are most successful in this space think of this process as a 'cycle' or 'loop'. Customers misbehave and innovate with a product, companies identify and enable the resulting innovation, and customers start the process over again. The terms most often associated with customer activities on our products, especially digital products, are *co-creation* and *co-production*. Co-creation refers to users constructing their own experiences through personalized interaction.[8] An easy way to think of co-creation is in terms of user-generated content on a social networking site, or in terms of content creation in the form of comments left on a blog. Users co-create when they add comments to an article on a news site, or when they post status updates on LinkedIn or Facebook. They also co-create when they use the existing features of a site, in a fashion intended by the product owners, to personalize their interactions. Following specific people on Twitter, for instance, is an act of co-creation. In our eBay Motors example, when a seller listed an item for sale within the right category (for instance a Beanie Baby listed in the Beanie Baby category), they were involved in an act of co-creation.

Co-production is the activity of contributing or modifying the product or service offering itself.[9] We very often use the term *misuse* as a special type of co-production when that co-production is not specifically invited by the company producing the product. Misuse is the result of customer's *misbehaving* when performing uninvited co-production. Listing a high dollar value Ferrari for sale on eBay at a time when eBay was not intended to support such a sale is an example both of *co-production* and more specifically *misuse* or customer *misbehavior*. Creating an extension to an audio player such as an iPod Nano so that it can be worn as a watch is another example of customer misbehavior and co-production as the watchband extends the product offering.

Our research indicates that co-creation is an antecedent to co-production. Intuitively, it makes sense that a product would first need to be used and understood (or consumed) before it can be augmented or extended.[10] The seller of the Ferrari likely either had prior experience with eBay in using it to sell items, or had his wife (a frequent seller) help him in his efforts to list his item for sale in a new and unexpected way. The iWatchz team had to have some experience in the

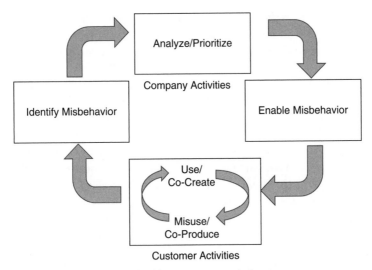

Figure 3.1 *Virtuous Cycle of Customer Misbehavior*

capabilities of the iPod Nano (that is, knew that it offered a clock and that it had a clip) to patent its special band and fastener to make it into a watch.

We can now describe a virtuous cycle of customers misbehaving and innovating on behalf of a company, and a company identifying and enabling that misbehavior. Figure 3.1 displays this cycle. The bottom of the cycle shows customers engaged in co-creation of the product (usage of the product), with some small portion of them involved in a cycle of both creation and production. The top of the cycle displays the successful company involved in a cycle of identifying, analyzing, prioritizing, and then enabling some subset of the new innovations.

So far in this chapter we have discussed the virtuous cycle of co-production and company enablement, leading to value-creating product innovation. Before we put these concepts together to describe how they interact in a larger model of value creation, let's first highlight a few pitfalls that can bring the virtuous cycle of Figure 3.1 to a full stop.

'SHUT DOWN THAT MISBEHAVIOR!'

In Chapter 8 we share some stories of how companies kill the virtuous cycle identified in Figure 3.1. But we thought it important to highlight some of the key pitfalls here as they are so very important to whether a product is allowed an opportunity to create viral growth.

Some companies simply never identify emergent customer behaviors. When the customer base is large, and only a small number of users are using a product in an unforeseen way, it is easy to see that the activities may be overlooked. In these cases, the activity never truly has an opportunity to flourish and has the possibility of dying before being enabled.

Research on 'lead users' (another name for our misbehaving customers) shows that companies very often will discount the value of the new and innovative usage.[11] It is common to fall into the trap of thinking that just because only a handful (and sometimes only one) user is attempting to use our product in an unforeseen way, there simply isn't a market demand for it. These companies identify the misbehavior (the left-side of Figure 3.1), but stop it in the analysis phase. An outside contribution to innovation in these cases is effectively killed and the virtuous cycle is stopped.

Another common failure in the analysis phase of Figure 3.1 is to favor internal innovation over external innovation. Companies may fall back on processes designed to analyze and prioritize internal concepts first, or favor those ideas that are most closely tied to current market thinking and approaches or processes.[12] Returning to the eBay story, the struggles that Simon Rothman had inside eBay in attempting to launch eBay Motors is a good example of this. The eBay processes at the time were developed using a manufacturing metaphor focused on maximizing developer throughput (or maximizing the amount of work a software developer would produce). The product backlog of new ideas was closely watched, and developer progress through this backlog closely monitored. The result was a very efficient product development process, but not one that could always respond well to new market shifts. This isn't an eBay problem specifically, it is one that research has shown time and time again happens in many product companies across multiple industries.[13] Companies with this type of failure effectively identify and analyze customer misbehavior, but ineffectively execute upon it due to processes that bias their decisions.

One additional failure somewhat akin to failing to properly prioritize is for companies to, in tunnel vision fashion, simply pursue their own agenda. The key difference here is that these companies see the emergent customer co-production as 'misuse' or 'customer misbehavior' (hence the name of this book). These companies aggressively monitor for such behavior, but never analyze it, to understand the potential, or prioritize it; they simply immediately try to put an end to it. The use isn't seen as just inconsistent with the original product vision – it is seen as destructive and an impedance to the true destiny of the product. There are of course cases where this should happen, such as the case of fraudulent activities in payment processors. A key lesson from both our research and the research on 'lead users' is that companies should actively monitor for misbehavior and then properly analyze and priori-tize it before taking action.[14]

Now let's take a look at how the concepts we've described above interact to create a model of viral growth.

BUILDING THE VIRAL MISBEHAVIOR MODEL

Thus far in the book we have defined viral growth, explained why busi-nesses want to achieve such growth, detailed previous research that attempted to explain technology adoption, and now in this chapter we have explained how customer misbehavior can accelerate product innovation. Let's put all this together to create a model that we can use to explain how businesses can improve their chances of achieving viral growth.

Recall from Chapter 1 that we defined viral growth by stepping through the viral growth equation:

$$\textbf{\textit{cumulative users}} = (C_v * \textit{retention rate})^{(\textit{frequency})}$$

As we previously discussed, the term 'going viral' typically means having a viral growth coefficient (C_v) that exceeds 1.0, where C_v is defined by the equation:

$$C_v = \textit{fan-out} * \textit{conversion rate}$$

Because conversion rate within technical products is a heavily researched topic and covered in so many models from the Technology Adoption Model to Innovation Diffusion Theory, we focused on growth in terms of *fan-out* and *retention*. Ultimately, for a user to be retained they must have converted anyway, so our model accounted for this and treated these two elements separately. Furthermore we desired to understand how different components ultimately drove fan-out and retention, independent of one another. As a result, we chose to measure fan-out and retention as the proxy for viral growth within our model.

Our research indicates high levels of co-creation and co-production results in increased fan-out and retention. Variations in levels of co-production explained 41 per cent of the variation in fan-out and 14 per cent of the variation in retention (see research in Appendix B). Users who misused the product were much more likely to share the product with others and encourage them to use it. Users are incented to reinforce the acts of value creation in which they play a role.[15] In the case of the seller of the Ferrari on eBay, the person could expect higher value from their listing by sharing the listing with as many people as possible (fan-out), each one of them potentially being a bidder. In the case of iWatchz, the company is incented to heavily market their product and in so doing also market the sixth generation iPod Nano on behalf of Apple. The range of reasons why someone may use products in new and novel ways need not be pinned to the creation of economic value. Research has shown that people may misbehave with products to project aspects of their identity, or bond socially.[16]

As the Technology Acceptance Model and Chapter 2 suggest, *perceived usefulness* also showed a strong relationship to both fan-out and retention. Variations in perceived usefulness accounted for 49 per cent of the variation in fan-out and a surprising 56 per cent of the variation in retention. As originally envisioned within the Technology Acceptance Model, perceived usefulness continued to be an indicator of likely user acceptance, and subsequent behavior within our research.[17] The value of *perceived ease of use* was significantly less as a predictor of growth, but previous research has portrayed this construct as an antecedent of perceived usefulness.[18] Perceived ease of use showed great value in predicting the result of perceived usefulness, accounting for 41 per cent of usefulness' variation. Intuitively, the easier something is to use then the more likely a user will find the product to be useful. Often products or services that are difficult to use never get the opportunity to be useful, since people will not try them. For ease of reading, we will most often refer to perceived usefulness as simply *usefulness* and perceived ease of use as *ease of use*.

Figure 3.2 shows a partial model of our research results discussed thus far in a simplified format (curious readers can refer to the Appendix B for the full model, with statistically significant regression betas and significance levels of each detected effect).

The lower left section of the model shows the Technology Acceptance Model constructs of ease of use and usefulness. As described previously,

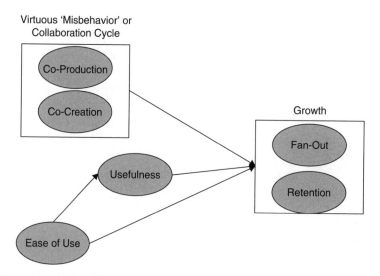

Figure 3.2   *Partial Model*

ease of use is a predictive antecedent (or has a causal effect) on usefulness. Together, they help predict our viral growth representation on the right side of Figure 3.2, which consists of fan-out and retention. Usefulness had a much higher relationship to these components of viral growth than did ease of use. The constructs that describe our virtuous cycle of customer misbehavior, collaboration, and innovation, co-production and co-creation (shown in the upper left of the figure) were also valuable in understanding the variations in growth.

Both the iWatchz and eBay Motors stories are great examples of the virtuous cycle of collaborative innovation fueled by customer misbehavior (represented in the top left corner of our partial model). In both cases, the product's usefulness and ease of use help to explain why someone would use the iPod Nano and the eBay service offerings. Both of these products were incredible success stories before either case of customer misbehavior. But in both cases, the attraction of customers to extend the product offering to new segments of the market afforded some additional growth opportunities to both Apple and eBay. In the case of Apple, it was the additional appeal to people who might want to wear the well-designed Nano as a watch – a segment of consideration not available without a mass-marketed watchband, built specifically for the Nano. In the case of eBay, it was a sizable additional market opportunity to participate and, dare we say, even help to revolutionize a segment of the automobile industry, consisting of hundreds of billions of dollars of gross merchandise value per year.[19]

But we shouldn't get lost in just the directly measurable effects of this model as displayed without stepping back and grasping a greater concept here. We WANT to build products and services wherein people are drawn to help us develop the product. There is an attraction here beyond the isolated case of a watchband for a music player or a market extension for a marketplace. There is something to be said about the magnetism of a product in which users will engage to help create value without direct monetary compensation back to that user. It is one thing for a user to ascribe value to a product, such as a watch, consistent with the utility that the watch provides. It is quite another for that user to engage, without salary, in adding value to that watch, whether it is in the quest for future financial gain or simply recognition of their contribution. When firms build products that incent such a level of engagement, and subsequently enable the resulting innovation, they increase opportunities for future growth at significantly reduced cost.

But this argument begs further questions: what drives customers to this level of engagement in the products that firms build? What product attributes help drive customers to want to help us extend a firm's product and service offerings?

THE DRIVERS OF CUSTOMER MISBEHAVIOR

Welcome to potentially the most important part of this chapter and thanks for not getting lost in the discussion thus far. Let's first return to the eBay Motors case and tease out the reason why the seller of the Ferrari used eBay to list his vehicle.

When Simon called the seller of the Ferrari, he learned several things. First, the seller was in a location that didn't provide great local demand for his collectible vehicle. Second, the seller was married to a wife who used eBay for buying and selling collectible items. Third, the seller indicated that he understood, from his wife, that eBay had an incredible nationwide reach where buyers and sellers were purchasing items 'sight-unseen', and shipping them to remote locations around the US and in some cases even internationally. These points highlight the *usefulness* of eBay to the seller of the Ferrari. A large domestic market could potentially overcome the lack of demand in his local area for his car. The seller had a wife familiar with the policies and operation of the site, making the site more immediately useable by him. The bottom line is that the site could potentially solve a problem for him and was therefore *useful*.

We can map a similar relationship for the iWatchz team. The sixth generation Nano shipped with a clock application consisting of a clock face that was displayed similar to that of a watch. It was even nearly the size of a watch, and Steve Jobs, in his presentation of the Nano, commented that a member of his Board of Directors was going to wear it as a watch (even though there was no watchband created specifically for it yet).[20] The Nano was clearly useful as a watch and only needed someone to create a watchband!

These two stories, along with qualitative analysis of dozens of interviews and evaluation of other similar stories, help confirm our quantitative findings that *usefulness* does indeed help incent users to engage in acts of 'misbehavior' and co-produce within a product and for a company. In fact, within our research, usefulness accounted for 43 per cent of the variation within co-creation. And as co-creation appears to be a necessary precursor to co-production, increasing product usefulness is incredibly valuable in kick-starting the virtuous cycle of co-creation and co-production identified in Figure 3.1. Figure 3.3 shows our extended model with usefulness now helping to explain how users are incented to engage in misbehavior.

Building upon the model of Figure 3.2, and reading this model (Figure 3.3) from the lower left to far right, we have *ease of use* as both

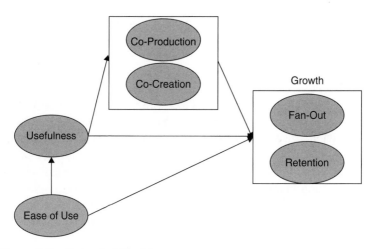

Figure 3.3 *Extended Model*

a small explanation of growth and a component of whether users see a product as being useful or not. The usefulness then drives growth even without the added effects of co-production (or misbehavior) as in the case of eBay without eBay Motors, and iPod sales without the iWatchz watchband. Usefulness also helps partially explain why users might engage in the process of misbehaving and ultimately co-producing with a company vis-à-vis the product being used. Finally, products that go through the virtual cycle of co-production – and enablement of that production – experience greater growth than those that do not.

While ours was the first research to incorporate the notion of co-production and co-creation as well as elements of the Technology Acceptance Model such as usefulness and ease of use to describe their combined effects on growth (vis-à-vis fan-out and retention), it felt incomplete. We struggled with why some products that were clearly useful never seemed to invite customer misbehavior, while others seemed to have evidence of such misbehavior early in their lives. Pouring through our initial qualitative research into social networks such as Facebook, Friendster, and LinkedIn, we found a potential answer. There appeared to be something about how certain products 'spoke' to people, or allowed them to display their individuality, that seemed to drive increased levels of co-production, co-creation, fan-out, and retention. Time and again, fanatical users who displayed high levels of collaborative activities, and who engaged in misbehavior resulting in innovation, spoke of how the products they co-produced allow them to promote 'who they were'.[21] We discuss this phenomenon (and its impact to the model in Figure 3.3) more in Chapter 5.

CONCLUSION

The companies in our research that met with the greatest success in viral growth engaged in a virtuous cycle of identifying and enabling customer misbehavior. The customers who engaged in such behavior appeared to be engaged in a cycle themselves, of first co-creating content with the product, then moving to co-produce the product itself. Sometimes that co-production manifested itself as the listing of a high-end collectors' automobile on a site envisioned to support the trading of collectible tchotchke items, and came as both a shock and a surprise to the company. Other times the co-production was not so much a surprise and was even foreshadowed as a possibility during a product launch.

Successful companies guarded against one of many pitfalls that can kill customer-driven innovation. One such pitfall is discounting the emergent customer behavior as 'too small a market to address'. Another common pitfall is falling back on existing processes, especially those that are 'internally focused' to drive innovation – essentially allowing existing processes – built to select and prefer internal innovation – to kill customer led innovation. Finally there is 'hubristic' pitfall; the classification of any usage inconsistent with that we originally envisaged as 'misuse' or 'customer misbehavior'. This last pitfall is deadly, as it assumes that only the builder of the product can innovate, and that the firm's product vision must be absolutely correct, even when market activity on or within the product indicates otherwise.[22]

Our research supports the notion that *ease of use* is a driver of a customer's usefulness of a product. Further, we found evidence that *usefulness* helps drive viral growth both in terms of *fan-out* and *retention*; the more useful a product the higher the fan-out and the higher the retention. Usefulness also helps to drive the cycle of *co-creation* and *co-production*, with products that are more useful having a higher probability of creating a desire on the part of customers to 'misbehave' or co-produce a product.

Thus far, we have explored the concept of viral growth and several factors that help explain the phenomenon. We started creating a model with factors such as ease of use and usefulness that help explain why users adopt any technology. From our primary research we introduced co-creation and co-production as explored through the concept of customer misbehavior. These additional factors help increase the explanatory value of our model of viral growth. The model still seems incomplete though, as we are now faced with the question of why users would misbehave and participate in co-creation and co-production. In Chapters 4, 5, and 6 we will answer this question by investigating the concept of self-identity and how it drives behavior – especially misuse.

Summary

- Individual users, and even other companies, can innovate with other firms' products and services by misusing them – using them in ways other than their original intended purpose.

- This customer misbehavior can lead to significant upside for firms that look to find and enable it. If eBay Motors only addressed 50 basis points (0.5 per cent) of the used car market in the late 1990s, it would mean as much as $1.75 billion in gross merchandise sales.

- Companies can fall into several traps and stall the learning process from customer misbehavior. Some of these include:

  ○ Dismissing the misuse as too small of a market.

  ○ Falling back on existing product innovation processes.

  ○ Outright declaring the misuse unacceptable and shutting it down.

- Our research indicates that *usefulness* drives growth and allows for the participation in *co-creation* of value with the product and *co-production* through misuse of the product. This in turn also drives growth via *fan-out* and *retention*.

4

The Concept of Self-Identity

In Chapter 4 we outlined our model of viral growth that includes the well-researched factors of usefulness and ease of use as drivers of such growth. Additionally, our model contained our newly-discovered factors of co-creation and co-production. Our research found evidence that not only does usefulness drive viral growth both in terms of fan-out and retention; but usefulness also helps to drive the cycle of co-creation and co-production. Useful products have a higher probability of creating a desire on the part of customers to 'misbehave' or co-produce a product. While this model does a nice job identifying factors that directly influence viral growth, we are left with the question: what are the individual user's motivations, beyond usefulness and ease of use, to participate in co-creation and co-production?

As we continued our research, a theme emerged about how certain products and services allowed the users to display their individuality. Time and again during our interviews, fanatical users who displayed high levels of co-creation, and who engaged in misbehavior with the products, described how the products allowed them to promote their self-identity. Self-identity is the last set of factors in our model. We are going to spend the next several chapters discussing the fundamentals of self-identity, how people validate their self-identity, and the myriad of ways that people publicly display their self-identity.

In order to understand self-identity we first need to review what we know about the social nature of humans. Humans as social beings desire interactions with others. These interactions often involve seeing others and being seen by others, such as working with others, going out with friends, or perhaps even interacting virtually in the online world. We partake in these processes largely as part of our ongoing existence and do not reflect on it much. We do this many times in an instrumental way, in order to establish and strengthen social bonds and linkages with people who hold significant positions in our lives. We partake in these processes with other people because, in part, these help us to form our self-identity, to establish the view we have about ourselves.

SOCIAL BONDING

Our journey into social bonding will first visit two types of rodents and investigate some of their peculiar behaviors. In laboratory settings, when virgin female rats, *Rattus norvegicus*, are presented with pups they will usually ignore or in some cases attack the pups. The mature females will only respond in a nurturing manner to the pups when introduced repeatedly over several days. However researchers found that when the same female rats were injected with high concentrations of oxytocin, a naturally occurring hormone in mammals, the rats began to nurture the pups almost immediately.[1]

Another type of rodent, voles, are small, brown, and part of the genus *Microtus*, in which there are numerous subgenus and species including the Montane vole, *Microtus montanus*, and the Prairie vole, *Microtus ochrogaster*. While these two vole species are similar physically, they differ in their mating habits. Prairie voles share elaborate tunnels and burrows, form long-lasting male–female bonds, and often raise young together. Montane voles, on the other hand, avoid each other except to mate, which they do frequently and indiscriminately, and often abandon their young after just two weeks. Montane and Prairie voles have similar levels of the mammalian hormone oxytocin, but the distribution of the receptors for this hormone differs dramatically. Researchers suspect these receptor distribution differences help explain the differences in the species' behaviors.[2]

So what is this 'love hormone', oxytocin? The word 'oxytocin' was coined from Greek words meaning 'quick birth', named so because of its uterine-contracting properties, which were discovered in the early 1900s. It is a mammalian neurohypophysial hormone that is believed to help mammals bond. Recent studies have begun to investigate oxytocin's role in various behaviors, including orgasm, social recognition, pair bonding, anxiety, and maternal behaviors.[3]

Researchers have also found that humans with higher oxytocin levels are more likely to trust other people and are more resistant to stress. Oxytocin levels in humans rise during childbirth, breast-feeding, and sex, as well as after simply being with someone we love.[4] Could it be that human behaviors and social bonding comportments are simply a response to hormone levels?

Aristotle wrote in *Politics*, 'Man is by nature a social animal; an individual who is unsocial naturally and not accidentally is either beneath our notice or more than human. Society is something that precedes the individual. Anyone who either cannot lead the common life or is so self-sufficient as not to need to, and therefore does not partake of society, is either a beast or a god.' Whether you believe 1) that hormone levels drive our behaviors, 2) that we are by our nature *social animals*, 3) that we are of freewill, or 4) perhaps any combination thereof, it is safe to say that humans require the social bonds of other humans to varying degrees.

Researchers have been interested in social bonds for decades, primarily stemming from the desire to explain social problems, such as crime and adolescent mischief. In 1969, Travis Hirschi developed the Social Bond Theory, which was later developed into the Social Control Theory.[5] The Social Bond Theory is attentive to the fact that social attachments are absent among juvenile delinquents. The definition of social bonding used in the theory includes four factors: *attachment* to families, *commitment* to social norms and institutions (schools, groups, and clubs), *involvement* in activities, and the *belief* that these things are important.

Not surprisingly, family, friends, and other members of our social networks affect our lives in many ways and we in turn are in part a result of their actions. One of the most critical times in our lives is our adolescence, during which we need strong positive social ties to represent society in a positive manner. If our parents work hard, providing a safe and loving environment for us as children, we have a nice head start to life compared to the toddler whose parents decided to set up a methamphetamine lab under their crib.[6] Surprisingly even the behaviors of people with three degrees of separation away in a network (i.e. your friends' friends' friends) have an effect on your behavior.[7]

Per the definition above of social bonding, the four basic elements are attachment, commitment, involvement in conventional activities as opposed to deviant activities, and lastly the belief in a common value system. We will look at each of these briefly.

Attachment

Forming secure bonds to other human beings fosters such traits as empathy and agreeableness. A securely-attached individual is more likely to understand the concept of respect and experience empathy, resulting in that person being less likely to engage in criminal acts. The formation of attachments can stand in the way of deviant behavior.

The understanding and implementation of respect is a social control that discourages disrespectful deviant behavior, such as vandalism and harassment. As Adam Smith, an 18th-century Scottish moral philosopher, observed the 'chief part of human happiness arises from the consciousness of being beloved'. In the original Social Bond Theory, Hirschi concluded that any type of social attachment was beneficial, even to deviant peers and parents. However subsequent research has found that attachment to delinquent peers escalates rather than diminishes criminal behavior; therefore the peer to whom an individual forms an attachment is important.[8]

Commitment

Commitment to a social group or organization fosters a sense of social responsibility as well as duty and honor to that unit. The military makes great use of this type of social bonding by placing individuals in units for extended periods of time – usually years. Commitment to a group can give individuals a reason to conform to socially-accepted norms and values. This sense of commitment for an individual can be a grounding force in their life.

As exemplary displays of commitment to a social group, we can turn to any of the US military Special Operations Forces (SOF) such as the Navy's SEALs, the Army's Green Berets, or the Air Force's Pararescue Jumpers (PJs). In Marcus Luttrell's book, *Lone Survivor: The Eyewitness Account of Operation Redwing and the Lost Heroes of SEAL Team 10*,[9] he recounts the story of his deployment with SEAL Team 10 on mission Operation Red Wings, to kill a leading Taliban member, thought to be allied with Osama bin Laden. One evening in June 2005, the team encountered three Afghan shepherds and a young boy. In accordance with the Rules of Engagement, the Team Leader, Michael Murphy, decided to let them go. Later that evening Luttrell, Murphy and two other members of the SEAL Team found themselves surrounded by Taliban fighters.

Adhering to the SEALs' unofficial motto of 'Never leave a man behind',[10] additional members of the SEALs Team 10 were deployed along with eight Army special operations soldiers. Their helicopter was shot down, killing all onboard. Luttrell was the only member of the team to survive and was rescued by a group of Afghan Pashtun villagers who kept him safe in their homes for several days before returning him to safety.

Involvement

Isolation from society can increase delusional thinking, depression, and suicidal tendencies. Involvement with others decreases boredom and feelings of detachment as well as carrying with it a sense of accomplishment and time well spent. Research suggests that social integration is generally associated with better health outcomes and that the quality of social ties also appears to influence the extent of such health benefits.[11]

Belief

Sharing a common belief system, such as attending religious functions, participating in political groups, or attending club meetings with other like-minded people, instills a greater sense of purpose. Emile Durkheim in his classic, *Le Suicide*, reaffirmed the influence that moral attitudes and beliefs have on the occurrence of suicidal behavior. Individuals with no religious affiliation were more prone to depression and suicide.[12] Durkheim, like Hirschi, believed that isolation is extremely detrimental to psychological development and therefore the participation in the social events of organized religion, as well as the belief system imposed therein, were beneficial. Perhaps no better summary exists than Durkheim's own words, 'The more weakened the groups to which [the individual] belongs, the less he depends on them, the more he consequently depends only on himself and recognizes no other rules of conduct than what are formed on his private interests.'

LINKING SELF-IDENTITY TO SOCIAL BONDING

Among both psychologists and sociologists, an emphasis on the multiplicity or multidimensionality of self-identity has led to the realization that it is no longer feasible to refer to 'one's self-identity' but rather it is necessary to refer to the working, online or accessible self-identity of someone.[13] The multitudes of selves that represent one's self-identity are not all available at the same time, but rather they are best understood as a shifting array of accessible selves through changing situations and contexts.[14] In other words, identity needs to be understood in relational and contextual ways.

The achievement of inter-subjectivity is the primary enabling feature of human communities where the self emerges through interacting with others. Self and identity come into existence through symbolic interaction in situated activities.[15] Thus we use social interactions to acquire and maintain our self-identities.[16]

We began building our model of viral growth with the well-researched technological factors of usefulness and ease of use as primary drivers of such growth. Through researching companies such as eBay and iWatchz, as well as surveying thousands of users of products that had obtained viral growth, we learned of the virtuous cycle of customers misbehaving and innovating on behalf of a company. We added this cycle into our model and were able to more fully explain why some products or services were able to achieve viral growth while others were not. However we were left with the nagging question: why are users motivated to participate in this virtuous cycle? Through more research we discovered that the ability to express and validate one's self-identity as well as observe other's self-identity was a particularly motivating factor for participating in the cycle.

In this chapter, we learned that humans are social beings that desire interactions with others. These interactions can occur in a multitude of ways that often seeing others and being seen by others in a variety of settings, such as at work, at home, out with friends, or even online in virtual worlds. Social bonding theory attempts to explain why our family, friends, and other members of our social networks affect our lives through four factors: *attachment* to families, *commitment* to social norms and institutions, *involvement* in activities, and the *belief* that these things are important. We partake in these interactions with family, friends, and colleagues because in part these help us form our self-identity. One's self-identity comes into existence through symbolic interaction with others in situated activities. In other words, we use social interactions to acquire and maintain our own self-identities.

In Chapter 5 we are going to look at how people use self-verification to reinforce their own perception of their self-identity. While we often use differences from others to describe ourselves we tend to avoid those whose opinion about our self-identity differs from what we want it to be.

Summary

- Our model of viral growth contained the technological factors of usefulness and ease of use as well as co-creation and co-production in our virtuous cycle of misbehavior. We were left trying to determine users' motivations for participating in this cycle, when we discovered the motivation of expressing one's self-identity and observing other's self-identities that derive from social bonding.

- Humans are fundamentally social beings. Researchers believe that individuals with no religious affiliation are more prone to depression and suicide. Durkheim believed that isolation was extremely detrimental to psychological development and therefore the participation in the social events of organized religion as well as the belief system were beneficial.

- Social bonding theory attempts to explain why our family, friends, and other members of our social networks affect our lives through four factors: *attachment* to families, *commitment* to social norms and institutions (schools, groups, and clubs), *involvement* in activities, and the *belief* that these things are important.

- We use social interactions with other people to acquire and maintain our own self-identities.

5
Identity and Self-Verification

It was early 2012. We were just finishing up our second round of quantitative analysis on what ultimately became the research foundation for this book. We sat down with one of our clients, Intuit, to help them with a project. This particular group within Intuit developed a platform called Live Community that allowed individuals to interact as a community around one of Intuit's largest products, TurboTax Online. Live Community allows users to communicate with one another by asking questions, posting answers, and rating the value of the answers posted to any specific question. The topic of our meeting was completely unrelated to our research, but the Intuit Live Community team mentioned during our conversation something that we just couldn't ignore.

'Many of the community members that provide the best answers to other community member questions do so under an alias', said Troy Otillo, the leader of the Intuit business unit responsible for the Live Community platform. 'What?', we said in unison. Maybe it was just the context in which we were operating (as we were there to discuss developing real-time business metrics with the team), or maybe it was as a result of all of our research to date, but this didn't sound right at all. 'You mean they are posting excellent answers under the name of their firm rather than their personal names?' 'No. They are using pseudonyms or avatar accounts. There isn't any link to their real identities, or the firms for which they work or own', responded Troy.

Later that evening, as we were having dinner, we started to discuss the reasons for individuals to provide valid answers for free without any attribution back to themselves. Our interviews and surveys with users of social networking sites indicated a great deal of strong identity-related motivations – including both voyeurism and exhibitionism. In our view, and given our research assumptions, the posting of answers to questions appeared to be an exhibitionist activity meant to expand or mold an identity within a certain social situation. It made absolutely no sense that someone would not want to have their valid and valuable answers attributed to their identities. Troy had indicated that many of the community members were actually Certified Public Accountants (CPAs), with their own tax return preparation practices. If anything, these folks should see TurboTax as a threat to their businesses – a technical substitute to their paid practice of helping people navigate the sometimes insanely complicated process of preparing their federal and state tax returns. And, if they didn't see it as a threat, surely they would want to use the platform to help drive customers to their own businesses. They should not be shooting at their own feet. Thus posting anonymously simply didn't make any sense at all.

'Unless', started Mike, 'it is because they want to limit their liability for answering something incorrectly'. 'Yeah', responded Marty, 'that has to be it. I think you nailed it. This is about protecting their business'. We could not have been further away from the truth. The CPAs hiding behind pseudonym identities weren't worried about the legal liabilities. Most of the question answerers had insurance that would protect them from such threats, and the answers on average were incredibly thoughtful and technically correct.

We had fallen prey to a common trap within any type of long-tenured research. When confronted with new information, seemingly inconsistent with our statistically tested and validated model, we started to look for reasons to explain away the inconsistency. After a great deal more research, however, we determined that the Intuit case was not inconsistent with our model. The masquerading users were in fact engaged in a form of identity project. Our research to date had been on the linkages of identity to social structure. But identity theory also has a vein of research focusing on the need for self-verification, to have others confirm that they see us as we see ourselves.[1] These individuals weren't looking to mold identities online within a social context, but were rather looking to have their identities validated.

IDENTITY AS A DRIVER OF CUSTOMER MISBEHAVIOR

The Intuit Live Community story, which we will discuss in greater detail later, helps illuminate the last piece of our Model of Viral Growth. Our research uncovered, time and time again, that products exhibiting the virtuous cycle of misbehavior/collaboration (reference

Figure 3.1 from Chapter 3), and viral growth often had features that allowed users to attempt to define their identities within society (Chapter 6) or self-verify (this chapter) their identities with feedback from society. These two paths of identity-related research are somewhat interlinked and are typically categorized under the label of *structural symbolic interactionism*, the goal of which is to understand and explain how social structures affect identities and how identities affect social behavior and structure.[2] Put another way, these two paths help to define how social structures and the perceptions people have of themselves work together to define each other.

This chapter explores one vein of research into self-identity: self-verification. The self-verification vein of research explores our individual need for others to see us as we see ourselves.[3] The theory posits that we prefer feedback from others that are consistent with the view we have of ourselves, and that we will actively engage in efforts to receive such feedback. The primary reason underlying this action is simple: the world is complex, confusing, and uncertain. This reality stands in stark contrast to our preferences for order, control, and certainty. In an effort to reduce confusion, increase perceived control and decrease uncertainty, we seek out confirmation that our hunches about the world (and ourselves) are correct.[4] The perception of coherent structure in the world around us provides us with both psychological and physical benefits; research indicates that the more structured and consistent the world seems to be with our views, the lower our self-reported incidents of emotional and physical ailments.[5]

Apparently this isn't how we are born. Starting out as a 'self-identity blank slate', we first attempt to define ourselves through the eyes of others. Children are initially concerned about how others see them, but over time they begin to adapt their views of themselves to the views of those around them. Later, as we mature, we try to ensure that the views others have of us and the views we have of ourselves do not change. This shift from conforming to others' opinions to later attempting to hold constant the opinions of others, and our own opinions, about our self-identity, highlights our need for constancy and reduction in uncertainty. Overall, people find confirmatory responses to be trustworthy and valuable whereas non-confirmatory responses are painful and felt to be less trustworthy.[6] We seek confirmation that we are who we believe we are in terms of skills, proficiencies, taste, accomplishments, social status, intelligence, religious beliefs, affiliation, and many other aspects of our lives. Many of the actions that we take in public places or online, at least where others can see us, are undertaken to solicit confirmatory feedback on our views of ourselves.

Negative responses in self-verification – those that do not conform to the views we hold of ourselves – often are followed with harsh actions on the part of the individual receiving the feedback. In many cases, individuals will cease relationships with others who have views dissimilar from their own.[7] Just as we remove individuals from our social network, we also seek out individuals that have a confirmatory perspective on our identity.[8] A third step we take in surrounding ourselves in a bubble of confirmation is to modify our approaches in interactions to ensure we achieve confirmatory feedback.[9]

With this primer on the self-verification vein of self-identity theory behind us, let's turn our lens back to the Intuit Live Community story and see if we can explain what's happening. The Live Community story serves as an example to integrate many elements of the viral model introduced thus far – including one additional element concerning identity.

INTUIT LIVE COMMUNITY

Intuit is a virtual hotbed of innovation and is widely recognized as a company capable of remaining highly innovative, even as it continues to grow in size and complexity along several product lines. Eric Ries, in his book, *The Lean Startup*,[10] cites Intuit time and time again as an example of a company that applies what we call 'fail fast and win big' strategies to achieve business success. Maybe it shouldn't have come as a surprise to us then that one of our longest-tenured clients would give us such an amazing and surprising case study that would ultimately help us expand our model and make it even more useful. But it did …

TurboTax is the leading online tax completion software available within the US today, and more Americans use the product to complete their state and federal tax filings than any other brick and mortar office/brand, online, or tax preparation software. The Intuit Live Community product started out as an experiment within Intuit's TurboTax Online product in 2006. The engineers at Intuit started placing 'in-product search' boxes on each page of the product workflow to help users find answers to their tax-related or product-related problems. The expected usage of the product was for users to enter a few keywords, just as they would do with a web search engine like Google, in order to identify and display Intuit-provided answers on key topics.

The engineers soon noticed a problem however. The number of 'no results found' for the context-sensitive searches on each page was higher than they had expected. In analyzing these results, they found that many of the failed searches included one or more sentences ending in a question. Users weren't doing what they were supposed to do!

Let's step back here and refer to our findings from Chapter 3. We know that for most companies, the answer to this finding would be to either train or badger users into using the tool *properly*. But Intuit is a unique company, in our experience, in that they focus on user needs and are unlikely to classify emergent unexpected behavior as either 'misuse' or 'misbehavior'. But even with this unique mindset, they are still subject to the same biases inherent to the human and company behaviors identified by Von Hippel et al – specifically to rely upon their views of what the product *should be* rather than reacting to observed customer usage.[11] Rather than fall prey to this trap however Intuit saw it as an opportunity to create a community and crowd source (à la James Surowiecki's *Wisdom of the Crowds*) answers to tax preparation questions![12]

Thinking back to our model from Chapter 3, Intuit implemented a feature intended to increase *ease of use* in creating a context-sensitive search system to help find tax preparation answers. Doing so, they opened up an opportunity for observing unexpected usage and analyzed the results of this behavior. They quickly identified an opportunity to allow for *co-creation* (allow people to post questions regarding tax preparation), resulting from users using the product in new and unexpected ways!

The Intuit team worked to implement a solution that would allow individuals to ask questions during the course of tax preparation and to further allow other individuals using the product to answer those questions. By carefully analyzing the results of each release of their product, they developed hypotheses as to what might increase *ease of use* and *usefulness* of the product and analyzed the results of their efforts with each release. Each release increased the interaction between question askers and question answerers. The Intuit team provided some answers themselves, but by 2011 of the 221,000 questions asked on the Live Community platform, 65 per cent were answered by non-Intuit employees. Intuit had innovated their way into what economists sometimes refer to as network effects business – a business in which an increase in supply (answers to questions) drives an increase in demand (questions) and both cause an overall increase in the total business value. In total in 2011, nine million users found 25 million answers to questions asked (unique questions posted to the Live Community site) or searches performed (searches for answers to a question before posting a new question).

This would be a phenomenal story of viral growth, worthy of inclusion in this book even if it stopped here. But wait, there's more! In analyzing the data within the Live Community platform, the folks at Intuit noticed that of the nine million users on the site, one in particular was responsible for a very large portion of the resulting successful searches (questions being answered before they were posted) and actual questions answered. This particular person, Intuit ID 'bwa', had answered nearly 84,000 questions and had over 11,000,000 views on their answers from question-related searches. It's important to point out here that 'bwa' is in no way paid by Intuit. Some 84,000 answers represent a significant investment in time on the part of this person. Think about it in these terms: if each question only took one minute to answer (undoubtedly answers to many of these tax questions took much longer), all 84,000 questions would take 35 weeks of work at 40 hours per week, with no breaks for lunch, coffee, or anything! This leads us to the question: why would they invest so much time on the platform without getting paid?

We know from our friends at Intuit that 'bwa' is a retired Internal Revenue Service (IRS) manager. His or her answers, under the lens of self-verification, could act as a continued personal validation of 'bwa's' skills and proficiencies, and a tie to his or her former profession and indeed to his or her self-identity as an IRS and tax professional. The Live Community platform has many mechanisms by which 'bwa' and other question answerers can receive feedback. Members can vote to say that the answer was helpful, vote that a question was solved, and even click a button to give the member 'thanks'. Each vote represents validation of proficiency, and hence identity within the platform. In fact, given the way in which Intuit calculates the 'success' of a search in answering a question, the search statistic alone (11 million and counting) is a validation of the power of identity verification and proficiency.

Our retired IRS manager, 'bwa', isn't the only one who gets such feedback either, some 150 members of the question answering community comprised of current and former accountants, tax attorneys, and even IRS employees, represent a vast majority of the answers and receive similar feedback. These volunteers toil without pay to increase the value and *co-create* content on the Live Community platform. Question askers also co-create this content and in fact, by asking questions within a keyword search tool helped to *co-produce* the platform. Intuit, by looking to identify opportunities of misuse, identified this co-production and enabled it within the platform to create an entirely new platform.

The engineers also created feedback buttons including the 'question answered', 'helpful answer', and 'thanks' buttons mentioned above. Initially these were intended to increase the utility of the platform, by helping members understand what other members found useful. An unintended consequence was the effect these buttons would have for building self-identities of the people answering questions. These buttons are, in effect, 'self-verification' buttons – a way for individuals to receive feedback that others see them as they see themselves. Interestingly, the pseudonym identities of the individuals answering questions create a bit of an 'anonymous' twist – reducing the price and pain for the question answerer should others not confirm their view of themselves.

Intuit isn't alone in identifying the benefit of identity verification vis-à-vis community interaction in their products. As early as 1998, eBay had created a community website that allowed users to interact. Much of this interaction was member to member, allowing members to post questions about policies, tools, and approaches. Members would share advice on how to increase sales, use the site in an effective manner, which options worked to increase sales, and so on. Our research supports the positive

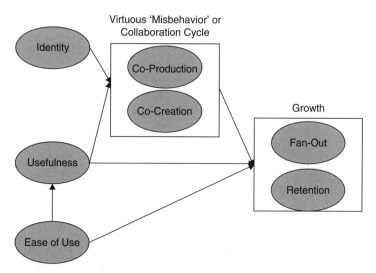

Figure 5.1 *Drivers of Viral Growth*

business effects for both Intuit and eBay by showing that there is a high correlation between the enablement of identity within a product and the creation of our virtuous 'misbehavior' cycle. Put another way, viral growth is highly correlated with the enablement of co-production and co-creation (customer misbehavior), and the virtuous cycle of customer misbehavior is highly correlated with the enablement of identity verification within a product. Figure 5.1 shows our newly-expanded model.

As we expanded our research into other, 'real world' technologies, we found further evidence of the self-verification of one's self-identity enabling a company's rapid growth. We found one example in an unexpected place.

CELL PHONES AND IDENTITIES

'Parents usually don't know how important a tool the mobile (phone) has become in young people's lives. They only think about the communicative function, not the social meaning.'[13] This quote from Gitte Stald's (IT University of Copenhagen) qualitative research on mobile identity is emblematic of the importance that smart phones have taken on in our lives – an importance that transcends their mere utility as a device for communication. Stald posits that identity through mobile devices is fluid in nature and that teens are in a constant cyclical process of negotiating and validating their identities.

In 2008 a Miami of Ohio student reported in the student newspaper that students had lost or damaged their cell phone on a roller coaster, in a rain storm, in a Frosty dessert, and by using the wrong charger. They quoted the representative from the phone carrier stating that 'someone recovered a phone after their pig had eaten it and that phone was in better shape than mine.' The student recounted that he had recently lost his newest phone and had to downgrade to a lesser phone for the first time in his life. He went from having a nice flip phone to his 'sister's friend's grandma's old phone, which had a black screen and five generic ring tones'. He felt like it was downgrading from a slick new BMW to an old mini-van. This student concludes their self-revealing article with the statement, 'Losing your cell phone for how ridiculous it sounds, is like losing part of yourself.'[14]

Stald's research and the student newspaper article are interesting for a number of reasons. Again, referring back to our model we see the elements of *ease of use* and *usefulness* in both. One girl in Stald's article specifically says, '... they made it so easy for us'. Both articles refer to elements of usefulness, from Internet access to social networking sites, to the use of diaries and calendars – our mobile phones give us access to the things we need almost anywhere we need them.[15] While smart phones definitely also allow for co-production, vis-à-vis the creation of applications to be sold and purchased within application stores like Apple's iTunes store or Google's 'Google Play', they also provide access to a number of applications and sites in which co-creation and co-production happen, such as social networking sites. Every element of our model is present, but it is the notion of self-verification of identity that intrigues us the most.

The Miami of Ohio student who wrote the student newspaper article specifically says that one of the hardest things to do with any new phone is master the ability to text at 200 words per minute. The words he uses, and the context within which he uses them, isn't about the speed of texting for the purpose of utility. He talks about 'mastery', and the notion that anything less than 200 words per minute is 'unacceptable'. This discussion is really about displaying proficiency to the outside world and the social network within which this student operates: about validating that others see him as he sees himself – a master of the mobile phone and its abilities.

Stald isn't the only researcher to find evidence of identities being linked to mobile phones. Cell phones have become a fashion statement for many.[16] This notion of fashion, self-identity, and the linkage they have within our theoretical model, are discussed further in Chapter 6.

THE NATURE OF VIRTUOUS CYCLES

For the analysis in our research we used a method known as structural equation modeling that is a statistical technique for estimating causal relations, using quantitative data and qualitative assumptions of causality (what factor causes another factor). When doing this type of analysis we build a structural or path model, where we draw paths from independent variables (i.e. those that cause) to dependent variables (i.e. those that are affected), indicating the causal relationships. If we create models with feedback loops they are defined as non-recursive and must satisfy special rules, such as the rank and order condition.[17] Additionally we must make the assumptions that changes in the system due to the feedback relation have already manifested themselves and the system is in a steady state. These assumptions are demanding, unrealistic, and there does not exist a direct way to verify them.[18] Because of this we often create models without feedback loops, despite the likelihood of their existence.

Figure 5.1 is a simplification of the path model that we developed during the course of our analysis of viral growth (the full model can be found in Appendix B). However we did hypothesize that a feedback existed between the dependent variable (growth – modeled by retention and fan-out) and the independent variables of identity and usefulness. For instance, as many products become more widely adopted, they become much more useful. Cell phones are a clear example of this phenomenon. As more people began to carry cell phones, it became more valuable (useful) for other people to carry cell phones so that they could get in touch with their friends and family, anytime and anywhere. Social networks follow a similar phenomenon – as more people join a social network, the value of that network (usefulness) to other people increases. This is known as positive network externality.

We argue that the same is true for identity within our model. Growth in usage and users makes a product more useful to display and validate identity. The most widely-used social network or product offers someone interested in verifying their identity the greatest possibility to do so. As certain fashion products take off, it becomes easier to identify with similar-minded fashionable people by wearing clothes that they wear.

One should also expect that growth in a user base will increase the amount of potential misuse within a product. The more people there are using the product, the more it is likely to be used in new and distinct innovative ways. Furthermore, as the misuse increases, an individual's ability to display their identity also increases. As such, we have hypothesized feedback loops from growth to misuse and from misuse to identity.

Our final model, presented in Figure 5.2, shows these feedback loops. Growth (adoption of a product through the factors of fan-out and retention) helps drive the ability to display and verify an identity, misuse within a product, and the perceived usefulness of the product. Increased levels of misuse help to drive identity within the product. For the sake of simplicity, the box encapsulating co-production and co-creation has been reduced to a construct we call 'misuse' and the box encapsulating retention and fan-out has been reduced to a single construct called 'growth'.

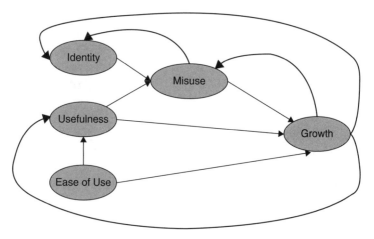

Figure 5.2 *Drivers of Viral Growth with Feedback*

OTHER EXAMPLES OF SELF-VERIFICATION

If you look around, you will find several more examples of self-verification enabling features within the products that you use. Both Facebook and LinkedIn have 'like' and 'share' buttons that allow others to vote on the value of a post or statement and share them with friends. LinkedIn also has functionality allowing others to vote and comment on various skills and expertise that a member may have. Twitter has similar functionality in its 'favorite' (similar to 'like') and 'retweet' functionality (a sharing aspect). Quora, a popular site to post questions and answers to various topics, allows people to 'vote up' the value of an answer to a question. Many of the social networking sites appear to have figured out the value of identity/self-verification within their products.

THE RAMIFICATIONS OF SELF-VERIFICATION ON PRODUCT DEVELOPMENT

Just as we should look to create products that are easy to use and that are highly useful for our users, so should we identify ways in which they can personalize their products and display and validate their identities. Creating a community around our products, as eBay did with its forums and as Intuit did with its Live Community product, is such a way to help users engage with their identities. Providing mechanisms by which others can validate an identity for a user, such as voting on the value of an answer, or 'liking' a post or comment, helps individuals to self-verify their self-identity. One corollary to this concept is that it may not be good for viral growth to allow users to 'dislike' something or for them to say 'bad answer' in a public way, despite all of us Facebook users, at one time or another, wanting a 'dislike' button. This approach may reduce usage on the part of some people and, consistent with the theories of self-verification, they may choose to leave the community within which they are participating.

CONCLUSION

The concept of self-verification, a vein of research within identity theory, helps to explain many of our actions. We seek out confirmation that others see us as we see ourselves, to help reduce uncertainty and confusion in the world around us. The need for this confirmation extends to how we select relationships, the people with whom we cease relationships, and how we approach topics in conversation. It even goes so far as to influence how we dress, the make-up we wear, and the trappings of our particular social status (watches, rings, bracelets, piercings, and so on). Our actions, such as texting quickly on a cell phone or providing answers for free to difficult tax questions online, may be as much about seeking feedback as they are about utility.

Many of the successful companies in our research enabled some form of self-verification and self-identity within their products. Intuit allowed people to both post questions regarding tax returns and answer those questions. Equally importantly, they created a feedback loop whereby people could confirm the views that question answerers had of themselves by voting on the value of the question and giving thanks. eBay had a community forum wherein users could post and answer questions about items for sale, how to sell items and how to be successful in shipping and/or paying for items. eBay's 'feedback' functionality is also a form of verification for both buyer and seller – buyers and sellers can post positive, neutral, or negative feedback about specific transactions with each other. Cell phones provide access to identity-related applications, serve as a token of identity (i.e. through their fashion statement), and provide a mechanism to display proficiency with a number of actions such as texting.

Self-verification (a method of managing one's self-identity) is incredibly important within our model of viral growth. Along with usefulness of the product, it creates an environment that correlates highly with the virtuous misbehavior and collaboration cycle of co-production and co-creation. Giving users an opportunity to display and validate their identities helps encourage their participation in user-generated content and innovative product development. Just as 'bwa' answered thousands of questions and helped millions of users with absolutely no payment, so too can you create products that engage with the identities of users to help incent them to innovate on your behalf.

This is not to say that the concept of self-identity is a necessity for the creation of a viral product. Our research does not support that conclusion at all. Our research only indicates that, of the companies we reviewed, enabling features that helped to project and manage one's self-identity seemed to be highly correlated with viral success.

Summary

- The self-verification vein of research in self-identity theory helps to explain why we do certain things. Specifically it claims that we:

  ○ Seek confirmation of our self-perceived identities from others.

  ○ Display actions, proficiencies, skills, and tastes that are meant to explicitly seek this confirmation from others.

  ○ Engage in tactics to elicit confirmatory responses regarding our identities.

  ○ Seek out partners who are likely to confirm our perceptions of our identities.

  ○ Remove partners who do not confirm our perceptions of our identities.

- Products that enable confirmation of self-identity are highly correlated with successful creation of the virtuous cycle of customer misbehavior, identified in Chapter 3. Thus 'identity' leads to co-creation and co-production, and is the last piece of our model of viral growth.

- Most cycles of growth, especially those that are viral in nature, exhibit feedback loops between growth itself and the factors that drive growth. That is to say that as something gains wider adoption (growth in users using a product) it becomes more valuable to others to use (ease of use). Growth also likely drives the ability to display and verify one's identity and the levels of misuse within a product. Increased levels of misuse help to define and verify one's identity.

- Companies should look to find new and innovative ways within their products to help enable self-verification. Examples from successful products include:

  o 'Like' and 'favorite' features.
  o Positive voting features (e.g. 'vote up' an answer).
  o Features that allow individuals to display their proficiencies, such as games of skill or ability.
  o Features that allow one individual to publicly thank another.
  o Features that allow individuals to explain or vote on the value of some piece of co-created content.

- Conversely, companies should be careful to shy away from features that are non-confirmatory in nature – at least those that are publicly displayed. Most successful viral products do not appear to have 'dislike' or 'vote down' buttons. This is not to say that bad elements of co-creation or falsehoods should not be removed – they should. But this is different than allowing others to vote something down or disconfirm an identity publicly.

6
Seeing and Being Seen

One of our co-authors, whose identity we will protect, is not what most would describe as a snazzy-dresser, unless his wife intercedes and picks out his clothes for some special event and then of course he looks very dapper. He's proud of this lack of style and when we began discussing how people tie their self-identity to their clothes, he was quick to point out that he must not be one of those individuals. Unfortunately for him, this isn't true. Our self-identity plays a larger role in many aspects of our lives than most of us like to admit – one of the co-authors especially. As the cognitive scientist, Donald Norman, in his 2007 book, *Emotional Design: Why We Love (or Hate) Everyday Things*, states, 'Even those who deny any interest in how others view them actually do care, if only by making sure that everyone else understands that they don't. The way we dress and behave, the material objects we possess, jewelry and watches, cars and homes, all are public expressions of our selves.'[1] This concept of using clothes, body art, or material possessions to display our self-identity is deeply rooted in the reflective level of the brain and highly dependent upon cultural norms.

When you notice whether someone's tie matches their jacket, or the brand of someone's eyeglasses, you are concerned with what is termed a *reflective self-image*. When we purchase something to support a cause, such as the yellow bands made so popular by the Livestrong Foundation for supporting cancer research, these are reflective decisions in that they reflect what we believe to be our self-identity. Even people who claim a complete lack of interest in how they are perceived, such as refraining from purchasing new items until their old ones are completely worn out, are making statements about themselves and their self-identity. There is no way of avoiding this process as long as you are not Robinson Crusoe.

In this chapter we will investigate how individuals use luxury goods (such as high-end watches, jewelry, and clothing), as well as environmentally-friendly products (such as hybrid vehicles), or even sports teams, to form and display their self-identity as part of social bonding processes. This is an important aspect of projecting self-identity and influences how we interact in specific situations.

SELF-IDENTITY, SOCIAL GROUPS, AND POSSESSIONS

People learn mostly about themselves from others, through both social comparisons and direct interactions. Researchers have found that one of the most powerful determinants of self-identity is the arrangement of the current social environment.[2] Individuals will focus on whatever aspects of themselves are most distinctive in a particular social setting: for example, short children will notice their height when in a classroom of taller children, and women will notice their gender when in a room full of male co-workers. These traits that are noticed come to the forefront of what one declares as their self-identity in that particular situation. As the character Nunez, in H. G. Wells' short story, *The Country of the Blind*, utters, 'In the country of the blind the one-eyed man is king.' Although as seen in the story (no pun intended), this stated self-identity doesn't necessarily prove to be true. Besides social comparison, how else can people form their self-identity with others?

Research shows that people, at least partially, form their self-identity from their possessions.[3] Viewed through this lens, self-identity becomes the assemblage of possessions; signals to define status, social involvement and stylistic intelligence.[4] A concept called *immersed self-identity* contains the combined influences of fortitude and social support, where the bond between consumers and their brands becomes so entrenched in the consumer's psyche that it actually becomes part of the their self.[5] The consumer intentionally has targeted the social environment, because it is consistent with, and supports, his or her self-concept. They cannot be whole without the brand as part of their life. In effect, the consumer immerses his or her self-identity in the social system of which the brand is a part. We can see examples of this immersed self-identity in several social groups but perhaps none to such a degree as sports fans.

SPORTS FANS

As Peter Eisler, of *USA Today*, stated, 'Marriages come and go, so do jobs, hometowns, friendships, but a guy's attachment to a sports team? There's a bond that holds the heart!'[6] Everyday brands that range from soft drinks to clothing to automobiles are finding it more and more difficult to sustain brand loyalty with customers. In today's world with information ubiquity, commoditized products, numerous alternatives in almost every product category, and strong foreign competition, there are very few barriers to prevent consumers from being attracted to alternative brands.[7] Interestingly research has shown that it is not satisfaction but rather getting customers to recommend a product or service that holds the key to fostering store loyalty.[8]

In the midst of all this brand unfaithfulness, one category stands out above the rest – sports clubs. Sports fans do genuinely seem to care about showing loyalty towards their chosen club or team.[9] Investigation of sporting fans indicates that the satisfaction/loyalty relationship is much more complex than in general settings, such as e-commerce or stores. Fans often remain loyal to teams during periods when the team is unsuccessful or performing poorly. Researchers have commented that although the view of all sports fans as unwaveringly and staunchly loyal is naive and idealistic,[10] the attachment of some fans to their teams is a central part of their self-identity.[11] Let's take a look at some sports fans to get a sense of how deep this alignment to a particular team is to the individual's self-identity.

New York native Spencer Lewis describes the New York Yankees as his religion – his *everything*. Demonstrating this loyalty he painted his car with every retired Yankees player's number on it, he owns Derek Jeter's game-worn socks, he has Boston Red Sox toilet paper, runs a business named Yankee Puppy, and he proposed to his fiancée on the scoreboard in 2006.[12]

We all have friends, relatives, or colleagues whose emotional balance hangs on their team's performance. If you work in a large enough office you've undoubtedly seen someone moping around on Monday morning due to a favorite team's loss over the weekend. Unsurprisingly, with an individual's self-identity tied to the team, losses can be devastating and can cause significant emotional pain.

When the San Francisco 49ers lost to the New York Giants in the 2011 NFC Championship, many irate Bay Area fans directed their rage at Niners' wide receiver Kyle Williams. Kyle fumbled twice in the game, including a critical punt in overtime that ultimately led to the Giants' game-winning score. One fan on Twitter with user name @javpasquel posted '@KyleWilliams_10. I hope you, youre [sic] wife, kids and family die, you deserve it' while another posted '@KyleWilliams_10 HOPE U RUN n2 A BULLET DA WAY U RAN INTO DAT BALL[sic]'[13]

With so much of themselves at stake, some fans just can't stand to stay on the sidelines and watch. In September 2009, a Spartak Moscow fan, apparently unable to stand the anticipation of a penalty kick, stormed the pitch and fired the goal past the rival's goaltender.[14]

On the more serious side, the emotional toll can be devastating to fans that associate so much of their self-identity to a sports team. Club de Regatas Vasco da Gama is a Brazilian multisport club founded in 1898 by Portuguese immigrants. With almost 20 million supporters it is one of the most popular clubs in Brazil. In December 2008, a fan threatened to jump to his death from the stadium after it was announced that the Vasco da Gama club had been demoted from Brazil's top division. Fortunately the police, along with some fans, were able to grab him before he jumped.[15]

Unfortunately things didn't end so well for a fan of the Arsenal Football Club, an English Premier League club. In May 2009, Arsenal lost to Manchester United in the Champions League semi-final. Seuleiman Alphonso Omondi, from Nairobi, Kenya, watched the match in a pub and became inconsolable, leaving in fits of tears after the defeat. He took the loss particularly hard, committing suicide just hours after the game while still wearing his Arsenal shirt.[16]

So what drives individuals to associate so much of their self-identity to a sports team? Indeed it is not at all unreasonable to assume that for some individuals a quest for social contact and sense of allegiance may drive their loyalty to a sports team, club, or brand. Individuals could become fans as a way to achieve group membership or be a part of a collective unit, the primary benefit of which is the sense of belonging that arises with group identification.[17] Collective identities are known for their ability to give individuals a sense of belonging to a group.

Researchers have found evidence of a 'social village' type of community amongst sporting fans, particularly when they view the sporting events from taverns, bars, and other commercial establishments. These are termed *third places* denoting that they are public places that host the regular, voluntary, and informal gatherings of people beyond the realms of home and work. Consumers identify a third place when the place is associated with the ability to satisfy consumption (eating food, drinking beverages, viewing sports, listening to music, etc.) and companionship needs. Associated with these third places are behaviors such as camaraderie, friendliness, kibitzing, and having fun.

Fans may follow the team because of the sense of identity felt by associating themselves with a particular group. It's easy to see why fans follow successful teams, in fact there is an acronym, BIRG, that attempts to explain this phenomenon and stands for Basking In Reflected Glory. BIRGing can be defined as the tendency of individuals to publicize their connections with successful others, when they have not contributed to the others' success.[18]

In a 1973 study conducted at seven large universities during collegiate football season, the apparel of students enrolled in sections of introductory psychology courses was covertly monitored. At each school, three types of data were recorded in the same classes every Monday during the season: (a) the number of students present, (b) the number of students with apparel identifying their school of attendance, and (c) the number of students with apparel identifying a school other than their school of attendance. The results of the study supported the notion of BIRG, demonstrated by the tendency for university students with no participation on their football teams to wear school-identifying apparel after their school's football team had won.[19]

But why do fans exhibit such loyalty when teams perform poorly? For this we need to revisit our discussion of mammalian hormones from Chapter 4, specifically *cortisol*. Cortisol is produced by the adrenal glands to stimulate gluconeogenesis (the generation of glucose from non-carbohydrate substrates to keep blood sugar levels up) and activates anti-stress pathways. It turns out that subjects in love have been shown to have higher cortisol levels. This condition of love-related hypercortisolemia may represent the somewhat stressful condition, or a general arousal, associated with the initiation of social contact. Such stress appears to be important for the formation of social attachment, since a moderate level of stress has been demonstrated to promote this kind of relationship, that is social bonding.[20] Other studies on groups as varied as military units and college fraternities have suggested that group bonding is reinforced as initiates undergo standard processes of hazing, resulting in significant levels of stress.[21] Sports fans that go through the stress of a losing season would therefore seem inclined to bond even stronger to their social group, increasing their loyalty and association with their self-identity.

Another possible reason for the loyalty to sports teams, regardless of the team's performance, is the differentiation that occurs through association. As we mentioned earlier in this chapter, our self-identity at any particular time is influenced by how different we are from others. One dominant purpose of collective identities is to define borders by differentiating between 'us' and 'them', thereby creating both opponents and solidarities.[22] This differentiation is quite clearly played out amongst sporting crowds, where fans supporting the same team will congregate together as a means of providing a sense of unity.

Loyal sports fans are great examples of this concept of immersed self-identity in a brand (the sports club or team) as well as bonding with social groups (other fans). It turns out that even not-so-loyal fans often want to associate with winning teams (BIRG) by wearing jerseys and other team paraphernalia. Of course loyal fans tend to don their team's colors through the good and bad seasons, regardless of team victories. Being seen wearing a particular team's colors is an outward display of the fan's self-identity that is associated with that sports team and social group. While sports fans are great examples of this public display of self-identity and social bonding, there are many more. We'll next look at a group of motorcycle owners who display similar behaviors.

HOGs

William Harley and childhood friend Arthur Davidson founded Harley-Davidson in Milwaukee, Wisconsin in 1903. Their first 'power-cycle' was a 7.07 cubic inch (116 cc) engine placed in a bicycle frame, but this proved to have too little power to climb hills without pedal assistance. Their next attempt produced a 24.74 cubic inches (405 cc) on a loop-frame design that transformed the motorized-bicycle into a new category of motorcycles. By 1920, Harley-Davidson was the largest motorcycle manufacturer in the world, having produced 15,000 motorcycles for the military during World War I. Being only one of two motorcycle companies in the United States to survive the Great Depression, Harley-Davidson went on to produce over 90,000 military motorcycles during World War II.[23]

In 1969, American Machine and Foundry (AMF) bought the company, streamlined production, and slashed the workforce, resulting in a labor strike and the production of lower quality motorcycles. Compared to Japanese motorcycles, the ones produced by Harley-Davidson were inferior and more expensive. Sales and quality declined, and by 1981 the company was almost bankrupt. That year, 13 senior executives, led by Vaughn Beals and Willie G. Davidson, bought Harley back and started the bike manufacturer down the long road to recovery.[24] These executives believed they could save the company by tapping into the fervent loyalty of its customers; the customers to whom Harley-Davidson was not just a motorcycle but an identity.

In 1983, leveraging the idealized lifestyle of a Harley-Davidson owner, the company established the Harley Owners Group (HOG) – a sponsored community-marketing club. Each Harley-Davidson dealership has the opportunity to sponsor a local HOG chapter that is supported by the national HOG group. Chapters elect officers from within their membership, produce a newsletter, and organize events such as rides, social gatherings, or even charity work. Today, there are chapters all around the world with over a million members in total.[25]

Besides promoting the Harley-Davidson brand, the lifestyle, and motorcycle sales, the HOG chapters provide a social group for individuals to bond with and form an aspect of the individual's self-identity. Members are psychologically linked to Harley-Davidson through the group that has distinctive values (such as, 'made in America') attributable to the parent organization. Members become embedded in what has been termed a *subculture of consumption* that has its own established practices, rituals, norms, and member expectations.[26] HOG members often wear Harley-Davidson apparel that distinguishes them as members of a group whose self-definition is linked to Harley-Davidson's symbols, products, and values. In fact, HOG members typically spend 30 per cent more than other Harley owners, on merchandise such as clothing.[27]

Riding up on a thundering motorcycle, decked out in a black and orange leather jacket with 'Harley-Davidson' emblazed on the back, is a declaration that you (and your self-identity) are affiliated with the motorcycle group. Are there more subtle ways that people exhibit their self-identity and membership in certain groups?

LUXURY GOODS AND TATTOOS

Bob Deutsch, founder of the brand consulting firm Brain Sells, states 'Luxury branding is not just about display, competition and comfort. It's about the personal exclusivity that comes from expansion of one's self-identity. Luxury experiences help to craft a "new me". With this new me comes new stories, and because identities are best understood through one's stories, people perceive you differently.'[28]

Researchers from the University of Rome conducted three studies in which over 750 individuals were recruited to buy fashionable watches, trendy backpacks, and cell phones.[29] The owners of cell phones were recruited in Rome, in front of phone shops where owners usually go to obtain products, and the non-owners were recruited among people walking in the same area of the city. Individuals were surveyed after their purchase to determine how much self-identity played a role in their purchase. These studies demonstrated that a concern over one's self-identity had a 5 per cent influence on the purchasing of Swatch watches, 7 per cent on the purchase of cell phones, and 9 per cent on the purchase of Invicta backpacks.

William James, the father of self-identity, stated in his 1890 book, 'a man's Self is the sum total of all that he CAN call his, not only his body and his psychic powers, but his clothes and his house, his wife and children, his ancestors and friends, his reputation and works, his lands, and yacht and bank-account.'[30] This role of material possessions in establishing and promoting one's self-identity has been reaffirmed in many academic studies, summarized by Belk, who claimed, 'we cannot hope to understand consumer behavior without first gaining some understanding of the meanings that consumers attach to possessions'.[31]

Fashionable expressions of one's self-identity aren't restricted to physical goods but can include tattoos and piercings as well. These body modifications can be seen as attempts to construct, maintain, and display a sense of one's self-identity by drawing attention to the body.[32] Current research estimates that the tattoo industry in the United States generates about $1.65 billion annually with between 14 per cent and 21 per cent of all Americans having at least one tattoo,[33] with more women than men having tattoos.[34] Of course, not everyone who gets a tattoo in their youth is happy with that decision later in life. In a study conducted at the Laser Dermatology Center, Massachusetts General Hospital in Boston, researchers found that patients there for tattoo removal had impulsively obtained their tattoos at a young age attempting to express their self-identity. Years later, they were now motivated to dissociate from the past and that previous self-identity.[35]

While tattoos, or the lack of tattoos, can certainly be an expression of one's self-identity, how do individuals express their interest in causes larger than themselves, such as global warming or the environment in general? Up next is the story of hybrid automobiles and why they appealed to consumers, despite the lack of financial benefits.

AUTOMOBILES

Having done an enormous amount of research in the automotive area that includes surveying over 50,000 people, Dr. Charles Kenny (whose company, Kenny & Associates, has helped GM, Nissan, and Chrysler market their cars) states, 'What we drive is completely emotionally driven. It's driven by ego needs and by self-identity needs. The bottom line is how does the car make you feel?' The story of the hybrid vehicles is exemplary of how self-identity influences our purchasing decisions.

In 2004, General Motors' Vice Chairman for Product Development, Robert Lutz, spoke to reporters at the North American Auto Show. Lutz was a legend in the automotive world, having a 44-year career, including stints as head of sales and marketing at BMW, running Ford's international operations and its North American truck division, and serving as President and Chief Operating Officer at Chrysler. He was an outspoken and colorful personality. 'A former marine, Mr. Lutz is a car magazine's fantasy of what an auto executive should be', explained a 2005 *New York Times* article. 'He chews on stogies. He likes to drive fast. He flies a Soviet-era fighter jet for fun. He thinks global warming is a bunch of tree-hugging liberal hokum and lives off the cuff.'[36]

Lutz had influenced the direction of hundreds of vehicles, and played a key role in the development of bestselling models such as the Ford Sierra, Ford Explorer, Plymouth Neon, Chrysler PT Cruiser, Chrysler LH sedans, and the Jeep Grand Cherokee.[37] In 2001, he was recruited by General Motors (GM), and given control over the company's product strategy, with hopes that he would invigorate GM's aging product lineup and regain some of the company's lost market share.

At the January 2004 show, several vehicles were showcased that Lutz himself had chosen, including the Pontiac Solstice convertible and G6 sedan. However reporters were passing over the Pontiacs for the new hybrid vehicles from Honda (with a version of the Accord) and Toyota (with the Highlander and Lexus RX). Despite this buzz, these were still early days for hybrids and sales were still anemic. In 2003, American car buyers purchased a total of just 47,525 hybrid models, compared to the Chevrolet Tahoe alone that had almost 200,000 units sold.[38]

To Lutz, cars like the Toyota Prius seemed a bit silly: 'It just doesn't make environmental or economic sense to try to put an expensive dual-powertrain system into less expensive cars which already get good mileage', Lutz explained at the 2004 show.[39] Lutz reasoned that as soon as customers did the math, they would discover that a hybrid vehicle cost thousands more than a conventional model, yet yielded only modest savings in fuel costs. Hybrids remained an 'interesting curiosity' for Lutz but he was confident they held little appeal for the average consumer.

Hybrid sales began to accelerate in the months following the 2004 North American Auto Show. Toyota had redesigned the Prius and demand quickly began to outstrip supply. Automotive journalists were also taking notice, naming the Prius 2004 *Motor Trend* Car of the Year. In 2004, hybrid sales rose 77 per cent to nearly 85,000 units. With gas prices at an all-time high, sales of popular (and highly profitable) full-sized SUVs and pickups, including the Chevrolet Sierra and GMC Yukon, were slipping.[40]

A year later, Lutz reflected on the growth in hybrid sales and GM's lack of hybrid offerings, standing by his argument that hybrids made no economic sense: 'It's not clear that you'll ever be able to recapture the cost of a hybrid in the pricing.' But he also acknowledged that GM had made a mistake: 'What we forgot in the equation', Lutz explained, 'was the emotional aspect of it.'[41]

Whether wearing a Swatch or your favorite team's jersey, whether driving a hybrid or a Harley, people want to be seen in a specific way in order to establish or maintain their self-identity. This behavior has been labeled exhibitionism, or digital exhibitionism when performed online such as in social networks. However this exhibitionism would not be satisfying, if not for people viewing these displays – voyeurs. Researchers ascribe motivations for exhibitionism on social networking sites to self-validation, management of one's self-identity, the development of new relationships, and the desire to exert social control.[42] Let's next look at why people create and share personal content online.

SOCIAL NETWORKS

Social networking sites have been around almost as long as the Internet has been a commercialized entity (arguably since 1995, when the National Science Foundation Network was decommissioned, removing the last restrictions on the Internet to carry commercial traffic).[43] Some of the earliest social networks include Bolt (a social networking teen community launched in 1996), Classmates (a social networking site launched in 1995 by Randy Conrads, to assist members in reconnecting with classmates), and Asian Avenue (a social networking site intended for Asian Americans that launched in 1997 and grew to 50,000 users by 1998).

Depending on one's definition of what constitutes a social networking site, the total number of these sites could easily reach into the hundreds. Sites are generally categorized as social networking sites if they provide services to facilitate the building of social relations between people who share interests, activities, backgrounds, or real-life connections. Usually these services include the ability to create a user profile, share information, pictures or videos, and communicate via email or instant messaging.

Ranking of the top social networking sites is also fairly arbitrary depending on what statistic you decide to use, such as unique monthly visitors, Quantcast Rank, Alexa Rank, registered users. However with more than one billion monthly users and 618 million daily active users as of December 2012 the current king of social networking sites is Facebook.[44] According to Dan Ariely, of *Wired Magazine*, the genius of Facebook revolves around the Wall, which is the profile space where users' content is shown and 'friends' feel compelled to comment on each other's posts.[45] A user's Wall is visible to anyone with the ability to see his or her full profile, and friends' Wall posts appear in the user's News Feed. Our Facebook Walls are a reflection of our self-identity on Facebook. Given the multiplicity of self-identities that we each have, our self-identity on Facebook is largely dependent on the social network that we have accumulated online. If we have mostly classmates then we work to display a self-identity that we want portrayed to classmates. If we have mostly family in our online social network then we work to portray a self-identity that we want associated with our relatives.

Researchers have shown that one can discern more about a person from their possessions in their offices or bedrooms than one can from spending time with them.[46] Therefore it is not surprising that we want our Facebook Walls to reflect our self-identity, in the same manner that we select and display our belongings for the same purpose. Researchers term this exposure of user-generated content that reflects our self-identity as *digital exhibitionism.*

Social networking sites offer individuals opportunities to constantly project their (sometimes highly imagined) self-identities. This often highly exaggerated 'self' has led researchers to assert that the physical body has become increasingly irrelevant in digitally-mediated social exchanges. Individuals are more free to construct their own likeness thereby becoming 'entrepreneurs of the self'.[47] A social networking site's value is therefore primarily determined by whether users reveal and build new facets of their self-identity to a growing number of other users who are watching. Multiple salient functions related to self-identity and social bonding are served by these processes of revealing oneself through user-generated content including: (1) self-clarification, (2) social validation, (3) relationship development, and (4) social control.[48]

Users who upload pictures, post comments, and update statuses, based on their personal information, are demonstrating digital exhibitionism. By participating in these processes of sharing, users hope that others will view and respond to their stream of displays. As Matthew Jones, Assistant Professor at County College of Morris, notes, such exhibitionism leads to content that 'is inherently more authentic and thus more intimate than producer-generated content'.[49] Overall, the character and consumption of user-generated content on the platforms is vastly different from that of content generated in traditional media.

Voyeuristic behaviors drive why users access the digitally exhibited content of others and engage in social exchanges. Voyeurism has traditionally been defined as a sexual disorder, or paraphilia, that involves observing unsuspecting individuals in sexual acts.[50] Recently, the term 'mediated voyeurism' has been introduced to reflect the consumption of 'revealing images of and information about others' apparently real and unguarded lives ... not always for purposes of entertainment but frequently at the expense of privacy and discourse, through the means of ... Internet'.[51] Thus people more prone to voyeuristic behaviors are also more likely to engage in the social exchange processes by monitoring and viewing the information about others. Indeed in the authors' own research we found that higher levels of voyeurism lead to higher levels of networking site usage.[52] Digital exhibitionism thus invites and requires its reverse coin of mediated voyeurism. This also challenges the traditional divisions between the public and the private,[53] as the increased ease of making personal content available records and presents individuals' mundane daily experiences extensively across social networking platforms. This also is changing the conventional code of what can or cannot be shown and to whom.[54] Overall this joint dynamic of digitally-mediated exhibitionism and voyeurism relies on, and encourages, the expansion of user-generated content and the need for related social networking services.

CONCLUSION

We've covered a lot of ground, so let's take a quick breather and put everything together before we dive into some case studies that will help cement the value of our model of viral growth.

The viral growth equation, defined in Chapter 1, helps us to define the levers for viral growth and establish a metric, or key performance indicator, for success. The equation addresses both elements typically related to revenue growth: growth in users (market penetration) and growth in individual user activity. Cumulative users (the total number of people potentially performing transactions) is addressed by the product of fan-out (how many users on average are invited per user acquired on our system) and conversion (how many of those invitations are accepted, resulting in new activated users). Activity is measured over a specified period of time (such as week, month, quarter, and year) by multiplying the cumulative users by the retention rate (those that were active during the period above) and raising it to the power of the average usage by users (number of times the average user used the product during that period). Fan-out, conversion, and cumulative users (and resulting activity rates) are all key operating metrics for measuring viral growth.

Chapters 2 through 6 identified key drivers of viral growth. Our model validates the notion that *perceived ease of use* and *perceived usefulness*, both adopted from the Technology Acceptance Model,[55] are important factors that drive product adoption. Both are therefore also necessary to achieve viral growth. Increases in ease of use and usefulness also correlate to an increase in fan-out and retention.

While necessary, our research indicates that ease of use and usefulness in isolation are poor indicators in helping to determine whether a product would go viral. Firms that achieved the greatest success within our research actively engaged in a process of identifying innovative customer 'misbehavior', and then enabled that behavior through product modifications and enhancements. Within our model, we call this cycle of identification and enablement the 'Virtuous Cycle of Customer Misbehavior'.

Implicit to this cycle is that customers first must have some way to help *co-create* value within the product or service. In some cases, certain users would then be able to *co-produce* the product or service; which we define as helping to actually produce the next generation of the product. We found that the best mechanism for customers driving innovation was through them using the service in a new or novel fashion, not previously envisioned by the firm, often termed misuse or misbehavior.

All of the successful companies within our research actively engaged with customers in this model of identifying customer misbehavior and then collaborating with the customer to build and expand their product. The resulting product would either help address new target markets, or help increase the ease of use or usefulness (and thereby increase adoption) within the current target market.

As described in Chapter 3, the identification and enablement of misbehavior runs counter to most firms' standard operating procedures. For those companies that do take action, it is too often the wrong action, tending to fall back and rely upon internal processes resulting in the rejection of external ideas.[56] Only when firms actively fight these innate tendencies and develop processes and guidelines specifically intended to enable external innovation (as 3M did to drive growth),[57] or identify and empower internal teams to champion such external innovation (as did eBay and Intuit) do they appear to be successful.

Usefulness appears to be correlated with our virtuous misbehavior or collaboration cycle, but alone it fails to answer the question of why some useful products entice customers to misbehave while others do not. The answer to this question appears to be tied up in the concept of *self-identity*. Our research indicated that customers are most likely to engage in innovation resulting from misuse when products allow customers to define and verify their identities in public, or observe other's self-identities.

Building upon this model, we recognized how adoption (*growth* as modeled by *fan-out* and *retention*) ultimately helps increase the value (usefulness) of many products. Growth in product usage also

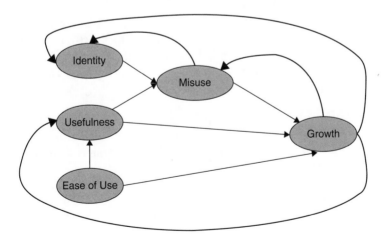

Figure 5.2 *Drivers of Viral Growth with Feedback*

increases the levels of misbehavior within the product, as more users are likely to mean more misbehavior. Misbehavior also helps us define ourselves, as we display our ingenuity or uniqueness through our actions. The resulting model (Figure 5.2) helps explain the virtuous cycle of growth feeding upon itself by increasing misbehavior, usefulness, and opportunity for identity verification and definition. These feedback loops help to explain the power-law growth that defines viral products.

In Chapter 7, we will investigate how to identify such misbehavior that can inform product development and how to properly respond. We will do so by looking at a number of case studies, some where the company accurately identified the misbehavior and took advantage of it and others where they classified it as misuse and tried to stop it.

Summary

- Self-identity is linked to social bonding in that self and identity come into existence through symbolic interaction in situated activities with others. People learn about themselves from others through social comparisons and direct interactions.

- Immersed self-identity exists when the bond between consumers and brands are so entrenched that in the consumer's psyche the brand becomes part of their self. They do not see themselves as whole with the brand as part of their life. Examples of this abound such as sports fans, Harley-Davidson owners, jewelry, and cars.

- Social networks offer people an opportunity to display almost any self-identity that they choose. The term *digital exhibitionism* has been used to describe how users project their self-identity through user-generated content.

- Digital exhibitionism invites people to watch and look. When users access the digitally-exhibited content of others, and engage in social exchanges, this is described as *mediated voyeurism*.

- In order to make products that people love and want to use, we need to pay attention to this motivator of self-identity. Great products allow users to display their self-identity through the use of the product.

7
Getting it Right

On June 3, 2006, a video uploaded under the username 'Eepybird' showed two men clad in white lab coats and goggles, dropping 523 Mentos mints into 101 bottles of Diet Coke.[1] The multitude of small pores on the candy's surface allow carbon dioxide bubbles to form extremely rapidly, producing a geyser of foam that erupts from the bottle. After posting the video, the creators told only one person, a brother in San Francisco, and yet by the end of the first day the video had been seen 14,000 times. Continuing to spread from person to person, this video went virally across the Internet, resulting in hundreds of millions of views by tens of millions of users. The two men depicted in the video, Fritz Grobe, a 39-year-old juggler/performance artist, and Stephen Voltz, a 49-year-old lawyer and performer, have appeared in their white lab coats and goggles on the *Late Show With David Letterman*, *The Today Show*, and at fairs and exhibitions on two continents. They have even spoken at TEDx, a local, self-organized event, modeled after the TED conferences that started in 1984 as a way to bring together people from three worlds: Technology, Entertainment, and Design.

Both companies whose products were involved, Perfetti Van Melle, makers of Mentos mints, and Coca-Cola, makers of Diet Coke, were quick to act upon this customer misbehavior by signing Mr. Grobe and Mr. Voltz to video production contracts. In October 2006, the pair posted a second three-minute Diet Coke and Mentos video, entitled 'Experiment 214', which was produced under sponsorship agreements with both companies. Mentos sales in the United States climbed nearly 20 per cent in 2006, their highest annual increase ever. This growth in sales continued for three years straight. 'It is safe to say the whole EepyBird Mentos geyser craze was a big part of the increase', said Pete Healy, the company's VP for Marketing. The first two video campaigns that were produced for Coca-Cola spiked sales of two-liter Diet Coke by over 5 per cent each time. Coca-Cola was so enthusiastic about

EepyBird's use of its product that it ran 'Experiment 214' for more than three months on its home page and promoted a competition to encourage people to submit their own videos. Grobe and Voltz have made dozens of other videos, including one with a Coke and Mentos powered rocket-car.[2]

Fritz Grobe and Stephen Voltz cashed in on the viral growth of their video, turning it into new careers for both. Besides continuing to make videos, in 2012 they authored a book *The Viral Video Manifesto: Why Everything You Know is Wrong and How to Do What Really Works*,[3] in which they provide four core principles for making a viral video. They propose that the videos must be real, get straight to the action, demonstrate something unusual, and have an emotional connection. As examples of these principles, they contrast a production-grade video of a couple proposing on a summer evening in Disneyland® Resort with the description 'A magical moment happens on Main Street, U.S.A.'[4] to the completely amateur but sincere *JK Wedding Entrance Dance* video.[5] The JK Wedding video features the wedding party of Jill Peterson and Kevin Heinz as they dance down the aisle to the song 'Forever', by Chris Brown. In the first 48 hours the wedding video was seen 3.5 million times,[6] as compared to the DisneyParks video which took three years to achieve five million views. By 2013, roughly three years after the launch of the JK Wedding video, it had almost 80 million views and was such a meme that the NBC television show *The Office* did a scene in the 'Niagra' episode modeled after it. The JK Wedding dancers appeared on numerous television shows including recreating the dance on *The Today Show*. There are hundreds of parody videos ranging from *JK Divorce Entrance Dance*[7] to one produced by the Norwegian Newspaper, *Sunmørsposten*, showing the employees of different departments of the newspaper getting together and dancing to the Chris Brown song.[8]

Coca-Cola and Perfetti Van Melle did something that few companies within our research did: they first identified the misuse of their products within the Eepybird videos and then *enabled* it. Within three months they had the pair under contract and producing 'experimental' videos that were promoted on Coca-Cola's home page. Other companies, such as McDonalds, OfficeMax, ABC Family, and Google, were quick to respond as well by sponsoring or partnering for Grobe and Voltz to produce other videos.

What if Coca-Cola and Perfetti Van Melle had responded differently? What if they had sued Eepybird for misusing their products or pursued a court order to have the video pulled down? It turns out that other combinations of candy and diet soda work as well. A 2006 episode of the television series *MythBusters* concluded that the potassium benzoate, aspartame, and carbon dioxide gas contained in the Diet Coke, in combination with the gelatin and gum arabic ingredients of the Mentos, all contribute to formation of the foam. A paper in the *American Journal of Physics* by Dr. Tonya Coffey at Appalachian State University, agreed with many of the *MythBusters* findings, concluding that the contact angle of these ingredients 'reduce the work required for bubble formation, allowing carbon dioxide to rapidly escape from the soda' and that other candy such as Wint-o-green Lifesavers® or mixtures of baking soda and water would also work.[9] Had Coca-Cola and Perfetti Van Melle responded negatively to the video, it is likely that another diet soda and candy manufacturer would have been used and they would have received the name brand recognition and increase in sales.

The Eepybird story is a great example of how companies can quickly identify and take advantage, for marketing purposes, of the opportunity produced by customer misbehavior. Coca-Cola and Perfetti Van Melle didn't change their soda or candy formula based on this misuse but they did encourage the behavior, which had huge positive results in their product sales for several years. In the remainder of this chapter we will investigate how companies in very different industries identified customer misbehavior, leveraging it for the benefit of their brands and resulting in greater sales or adoption of their products and services.

EVENTS – FACEBOOK

Let's turn from viral videos of diet soda and candy to Internet-based social networking services. As noted previously, Facebook demonstrated viral growth patterns and was ranked in 2009 as the most used social network worldwide by monthly active users[10] with over 955 million users by June 2012.[11] See Figure 7.1, which graphically represents Facebook's growth.

In 2008, the fastest growing demographic was age 25+,[12] but by 2009 it was an age cohort of 35–54 year olds,[13] and by 2012 it was 45–54 year-olds.[14] Facebook's retention has been strong, with 552 million users updating their status each day,[15] and users spending an average of 405 minutes on the site per month.[16] In addition, mechanisms introduced to allow users to automatically invite friends have led to effectiveness of these social-media-organized revolutions, all but one of the protests called for on Facebook ended up coming to life on the streets.[32] On Twitter, hashtags (the number sign # followed by a term) are used to identify the subject of tweets making it easy to retrieve these tweets during searches for a particular term. The hashtag #Egypt had 1.4 million mentions in the three months with #Libya having 990,000 and #protest having 620,000. How was Twitter able to establish the functionality that allowed it to not only have such a huge impact on individuals' social networks but also on entire countries and governments? Was there a product genius who envisioned this? The answer, as was the case with Facebook, is 'No'. The 'genius' of these companies is not an individual employee but rather is embedded within the collective innovative misuse of their products by their customer base.

Twitter co-founder Evan Williams, at a 2009 TED talk,[33] stated, 'The fundamental idea is that Twitter lets people share moments of their lives whenever they want – be they momentous occasions or mundane ones. It is by sharing these moments as they are happening that lets people feel more connected and in touch despite distance and in real time. This is the primary use we saw of Twitter from the beginning and what got us excited. What we didn't anticipate was the many, many other uses that would evolve from this very simple system.' Williams went on to describe the use of Twitter by news agencies such as the *LA Times* during emergencies to provide instant updates, and the use by an insanely popular Korean-barbecue truck that posts its location, causing people to line up around the block. He also describes how users helped evolve the product by finding a way to respond to posts by other users using the @username in a post. That was 'completely invented by users, we didn't build into the system until it became popular and then we made it easier'. See Figure 7.2 as an example of how one of the authors is using the @username to congratulate ObjectRocket and its founders (Chris Lalonde, Erik Beebe, and Kenny Gorman) on its acquisition by Rackspace in the top tweet, and congratulating two employees of *The Guardian* on an article highlighting the newspaper's growth of digital audience in the bottom tweet.

But what about the hashtag that was used so widely during the Arab Spring to allow protestors to find each other and coordinate participation in events? Williams goes on to state about the invention of the hashtag used in searching:

> Probably the most important third party development came from a little company in Virginia called Summize. Summize

built a Twitter search engine. They tapped into the fact that if you have millions of people around the world talking about what they are doing and what is happening around them you have an incredible resource to find out what's happen among any topic or event while it is going on. This really changed how we perceived Twitter ... this is another way that our mind has shifted and Twitter wasn't really originally what we thought it was.

Figure 7.2   *Hashtag Example*

No doubt, the original idea for Twitter was the brainchild of one individual, nurtured by a few others, and developed by hundreds of engineers. However, much of the innovation that has made it so impactful for individuals as well as society has come from users 'misbehaving' with the product. Users took a very simple tool and turned it into what they needed at the time. They needed to respond to each other so they came up with the @username. They needed to be able to find each other's tweets easily so they came up with hashtags and a search engine. This is a classic example of co-production by users and a terrific example of a company that was wise enough to let users explore and misuse the product. Had Jack Dorsey or Evan Williams said 'this isn't what I envisioned' and stopped the users from creating these amazing pieces of functionality, it is very likely that Twitter would not have achieved the growth that it has nor would it have had such an impact.

If we check Twitter against our viral growth model we see, similar to Facebook, that they were successful with all the constructs necessary for viral growth. The interface was simple and easy to use, it was useful in a number of ways, it allowed users to express their self-identity, and others to consume it and provide feedback. The entirety of the value of Twitter is the content co-created by the users and lastly they not only

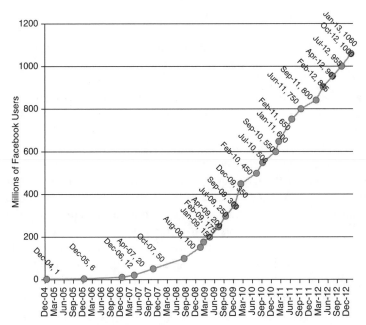

Figure 7.1   *Facebook Growth*[17]

significant fan-out rates: the average Facebook user currently has about 100 friends. How did Facebook achieve such phenomenal growth, with high levels of fan-out, conversion, and retention?

First and foremost, Facebook is fervent about growth, and almost since the founding of the company there has been a dedicated growth team that receives specific attention from Zuckerberg and his top management team.[18] This fanatical attention to growth factors has allowed the Facebook team to tweak the service offerings, ranging from features such as a Friend Finder (enabled by importing contacts)[19] to the site's user privacy policy.[20]

If we use our viral growth model we can highlight some of the factors that were helping Facebook achieve such phenomenal growth. Starting with the concept of *easy to use*, one can argue that Facebook from the start has had a simple, clean design that aided usability. While it is likely that in the early days of Facebook the main focus was functionality over user interface, nonetheless Zuckerberg has given some insight into his design considerations stating, 'Since the early days, simplicity has been at the heart of Facebook.'[21] In our survey of 1449 users of eight social networks (see Appendix A), we found that Facebook had the highest normalized score (potential range between −1.00 and +1.00) of 0.18 for the construct of *perceived ease of use*, whereas other social networks such as Friendster had a −0.89 score.

The usefulness of Facebook as a social network is also fairly easy to argue as it had the benefit of defining much of the functionality that constitutes a social network. We also see from the early days the functionality to post profiles, relationship status, and even profile images, all of which proved useful but also provided for individuals to exhibit the self-identity of their making. As voyeuristic viewing of other people's profiles was one of the primary purposes of the platform, 'poking' was an early piece of functionality that allowed one user to know another user was watching or thinking about them. Additionally there were some privacy controls even in the earliest versions that would limit who could view your profile (friends only, only people in my class year). These all add up to users being able to create and manage their self-identity as well as receive encouragement from others. As the users added more metadata into their profiles and status updates, which became available in September 2006, they were co-creating value on the platform.

Thus far we see that Facebook was being successful with the platform's ease of use, usefulness, self-identity, and even co-creation of value through the user-generated content. All of these are necessary in our model to achieve viral growth, and Facebook was meeting all of them. The last piece in our model is enabling the co-production of the platform itself through customer misbehavior. As it turns out, Facebook engineers and product managers were watching customer misbehavior and learning from it.

Chris Cox, VP of Product at Facebook, relayed this story in his closing remarks of the 2010 F8 Developer Conference. When Facebook launched its 'friend' feature, students used the profile feature to 'friend' fraternities and classes. The Facebook team thought it didn't make sense to 'friend' a class so they built the 'groups' feature. This feature, in addition to being used for clubs, classes, and teams, started to be used for parties. Parties, unlike fraternities, needed start times so Facebook built 'my parties', which eventually evolved into its 'events' feature. Cox described the Facebook approach as 'watch[ing] users misuse what we had already given them and build[ing] the product that captured what they want to do'. This practice stands in stark contrast to the approach used by a competitor, which we will discuss in Chapter 8.

In interviews that the authors conducted, former Facebook employees discussed how Facebook was focused from inception on viral growth, adopting a strategy of relentless vigilance towards its users. As one executive revealed, 'growing [was always] the most important thing'. To fuel growth, engineers observed and relied upon feedback from users for product strategy. Chris Cox, in a blog post dated 24 March 2009, in response to Facebook's home page redesign, stated: 'We listen to feedback from our users, data on how the site is used, and our intuitions as builders and designers, to create the product that provides the best experience across the board.'[22] Facebook continuously *watched* how users used, and of course misused, their products by gathering usage data. These data guided their product development roadmap and helped ensure they were building features or making changes to their services that would encourage users to recommend the service to others (fan-out) and continue using it themselves (retention). Let's continue looking at Internet-based social networking services that have done a great job of paying attention to user misbehavior, and leveraging it to achieve viral growth.

TWITTER

Twitter is an Internet-based social networking service known as a 'micro-blogging' service. Users can post and read text-based messages (limited to 140 characters) that are known as 'tweets'. Twitter was co-founded by Jack Dorsey, Noah Glass, Evan Williams, and Biz Stone during a brainstorming session held by Board members of the podcasting company Odeo. Jack Dorsey, at the time an undergraduate student at New York University, was sitting on a children's slide eating Mexican food when he suggested a simple way to send status updates by using text messages.[23] The side project, originally code named 'twttr', which was inspired by the five-character length of American SMS short codes, was prototyped in March 2006 to be used as an internal service for Odeo employees. The full version was introduced publicly on 15 July 2006. The service rapidly gained worldwide popularity, with over 500 million registered users as of 2012, generating over 340 million tweets and over 1.6 billion searches per day.[24]

The first tipping point for Twitter's popularity, arguably, was the 2007 South by Southwest Interactive (SXSWi) conference, during which Twitter placed two 60-inch plasma screens in the conference hallways streaming Twitter messages. Panelists and speakers mentioned the service and the bloggers touted it, resulting in Twitter usage increasing from 20,000 tweets per day to 60,000.[25] These massive spikes in usage have been typical for Twitter, primarily around prominent news, sports, or entertainment events. Twitter grew in 2009 at a staggering 1382 per cent on an annual basis,[26] which drove it into the position of 3rd highest-ranking social networking site in January 2009, from its previous ranking of 22nd.[27] Besides driving user adoption, these spikes have occasionally caused service interruptions. When the news of Michael Jackson's death was reported, users began tweeting with the words 'Michael Jackson' in their posts at a rate of 100,000 tweets per hour, causing Twitter's servers to crash.[28]

Twitter has had a large impact on individuals and businesses as an Internet social network, based on the numbers of users and amount of content generated, but its role in shaping social events is perhaps even more interesting. The Arab Spring is a revolutionary wave of demonstrations, protests, and wars that began in December 2010 in the Arab world. Major protests broke out in Algeria, Iraq, Jordan, Kuwait, Morocco, and Sudan. As a direct result of these actions rulers have been forced from power in Tunisia, Egypt, Libya, and Yemen.[29] While protests and revolts have occurred in the Arab states since the 1800s, this round of intense riots and protests was initiated by the self-immolation of one Tunisian, Mohamed Bouazizi. Unable to find work, he resorted to selling fruit at a roadside stand, until a municipal inspector confiscated his goods on 17 December. An hour later he doused himself with gasoline and set himself afire.

His death sparked the Tunisian revolution by bringing together various groups, ranging from the unemployed to political and human rights activists to professors, all of whom were dissatisfied with the existing system.[30] With the success of the protests in Tunisia, a wave of unrest struck Algeria, Jordan, Egypt, and Yemen then spread to other countries. During these protests, social media such as Facebook, Twitter, and YouTube, have taken on various roles in coordinating and documenting the events. One activist tweeted during the days of protests in Cairo, 'We use Facebook to schedule the protests, Twitter to coordinate, and YouTube to tell the world', explaining why social media was so important to the organization of political unrest.[31]

Nearly 90 per cent of Egyptians and Tunisians, surveyed in March 2011, said they were using Facebook to organize or spread awareness about protests. While detractors and government officials denied the effectiveness of these social-media-organized revolutions, all but one of the protests called for on Facebook ended up coming to life on the streets.[32] On Twitter, hashtags (the number sign # followed by a term) are used to identify the subject of tweets making it easy to retrieve these tweets during searches for a particular term. The hashtag #Egypt had 1.4 million mentions in the three months with #Libya having 990,000 and #protest having 620,000. How was Twitter able to establish the functionality that allowed it to not only have such a huge impact on individuals' social networks but also on entire countries and governments? Was there a product genius who envisioned this? The answer, as was the case with Facebook, is 'No'. The 'genius' of these companies is not an individual employee but rather is embedded within the collective innovative misuse of their products by their customer base.

Twitter co-founder Evan Williams, at a 2009 TED talk,[33] stated, 'The fundamental idea is that Twitter lets people share moments of their lives whenever they want – be they momentous occasions or mundane ones. It is by sharing these moments as they are happening that lets people feel more connected and in touch despite distance and in real time. This is the primary use we saw of Twitter from the beginning and what got us excited. What we didn't anticipate was the many, many other uses that would evolve from this very simple system.' Williams went on to describe the use of Twitter by news agencies such as the *LA Times* during emergencies to provide instant updates, and the use by an insanely popular Korean-barbecue truck that posts its location, causing people to line up around the block. He also describes how users helped evolve the product by finding a way to respond to posts by other users using the @username in a post. That was 'completely invented by users, we didn't build into the system until it became popular and then we made it easier'. See Figure 7.2 as an example of how one of the authors is using the @username to congratulate ObjectRocket and its founders (Chris Lalonde, Erik Beebe, and Kenny Gorman) on its acquisition by Rackspace in the top tweet, and congratulating two employees of *The Guardian* on an article highlighting the newspaper's growth of digital audience in the bottom tweet.

But what about the hashtag that was used so widely during the Arab Spring to allow protestors to find each other and coordinate participation in events? Williams goes on to state about the invention of the hashtag used in searching:

Probably the most important third party development came from a little company in Virginia called Summize. Summize built a Twitter search engine. They tapped into the fact that if you have millions of people around the world talking about what they are doing and what is happening around them you have an incredible resource to find out what's happen among any topic or event while it is going on. This really changed how we perceived Twitter ... this is another way that our mind has shifted and Twitter wasn't really originally what we thought it was.

Figure 7.2 *Hashtag Example*

No doubt, the original idea for Twitter was the brainchild of one individual, nurtured by a few others, and developed by hundreds of engineers. However, much of the innovation that has made it so impactful for individuals as well as society has come from users 'misbehaving' with the product. Users took a very simple tool and turned it into what they needed at the time. They needed to respond to each other so they came up with the @username. They needed to be able to find each other's tweets easily so they came up with hashtags and a search engine. This is a classic example of co-production by users and a terrific example of a company that was wise enough to let users explore and misuse the product. Had Jack Dorsey or Evan Williams said 'this isn't what I envisioned' and stopped the users from creating these amazing pieces of functionality, it is very likely that Twitter would not have achieved the growth that it has nor would it have had such an impact.

If we check Twitter against our viral growth model we see, similar to Facebook, that they were successful with all the constructs necessary for viral growth. The interface was simple and easy to use, it was useful in a number of ways, it allowed users to express their self-identity, and others to consume it and provide feedback. The entirety of the value of Twitter is the content co-created by the users and lastly they not only allowed but actively encouraged co-production of the platform through misuse or misbehaviors. According to our model there is little doubt that Twitter should have been able to achieve an enormous growth rate such as it did.

Let's pause here and recognize another important effect within our model. Our research and experience with product companies that experience viral growth indicates that very often they run into problems 'scaling' their product infrastructure. User and transaction growth comes at such a fast rate that the systems, servers, and even the original product design have a hard time keeping up with the demand. Incredibly successful companies, including eBay, Twitter, and Facebook, have experienced growth-related problems that manifest themselves as slowness in response times or unavailability of certain services. These symptoms affect how people view ease of use and usefulness of the product.

Interestingly each of these companies was successful in continuing their growth in spite of these problems. They each took actions to address their technology issues as they arose and continued to monitor and enable misuse of their product. While we can't definitively claim that the enablement of *co-production* by these companies helped offset the damage caused by technology problems, it does stand in stark contrast to another company with similar technology problems and without such enablement that we will discuss in Chapter 8.

FARMVILLE

FarmVille is a farming simulation game developed by Zynga and launched in August 2009. It was an Adobe Flash application played on social networking website Facebook and Microsoft's MSN Games. Gameplay involves various aspects of farm management such as plowing, planting, growing, and harvesting crops as well as raising livestock. The game is 'freemium', meaning there is no cost to play but, optionally, players can purchase premium content. Taking advantage of Facebook's platform policies, Zynga incented players to invite friends to play and post status updates about their farms by giving them game credits. To some, this earned the game an unwanted affiliation with spam,[34] but also propelled it to achieve an incredible adoption rate. By the end of 2009, just five months after the launch, there were 69 million players of FarmVille, more than on the entirety of Twitter that year.[35] FarmVille achieved a peak of 84 million players within 15 months.[36]

Again, let's pause and view this growth in terms of our viral growth model. FarmVille, as a game, was incredibly easy to use, check! If we look at the usefulness of games as entertainment, distractions, and so on, then FarmVille again hit the mark. In terms of allowing users to express their self-identity, FarmVille also succeeded here in that each player could customize their farms and could display portions of their game play on Facebook. As the game was single player with multi-player interactions, the users actually co-created the value through their game play. The last piece of our model is enabling and encouraging the co-production of the actual product. Let's continue with our story.

As FarmVille and games like it grew in popularity, Facebook enacted a series of changes to their policies, potentially to counteract the concerns over spam. In February 2011, Facebook changed the way updates from FarmVille showed in users news feed.[37] At the end of July 2011, Facebook's platform policies changed to no longer allow game developers to incent players with virtual currency.[38] These policy changes combined with user access to Facebook migrating to mobile devices, negatively affected the fan-out and conversion rates for FarmVille. How quickly things changed for the company was underscored by the free-fall in the stock price from the Spring of 2012, when it was trading $4 above its initial public offering (IPO) price of $10, to a low of $2.09 by the Fall of 2012. Fortunately there were still millions of users playing the game daily allowing Zynga to collect over 25 terabytes of data each day. These data included how users played the game and were used for a variety of purposes, including customer service, quality assurance, and determining the next generation of features.

In the original version of FarmVille, animals were included primarily as decorations. The designers did not expect users to interact with the animals, but by scrutinizing petabytes of data about players' behaviors Zynga's analysts found that players were moving animals around the farm and using in-game virtual currency to buy them. Indeed, one user, Adam Hamnett of Greater Manchester, UK, was so desperate to buy virtual animals for his FarmVille account that he first robbed a blind man, Brian McKenzie, and then murdered Peter Boustead when his friends threatened to report the matter to the police. In August 2011, Hamnett was given a life sentence and must serve a minimum of 20 years.[39]

The Zynga designers could have taken the approach that this behavior was misuse and simply prohibited such interaction in the next version. Fortunately for Zynga and their customers, the designers did the exact opposite. In FarmVille 2, released in September 2012, animals were much more central. If you want to make and sell a cake, for example, you need a cow for the milk and a chicken for the eggs.[40] Since the launch of FarmVille 2 it has achieved over 40 million monthly users and over eight million players daily.[41] From 31 August 2012 to 13 March 2013, Zynga's stock price increased by 33.21 per cent – not returning to its post-IPO high but recovering significantly (see Figure 7.3). On their Q4 2012 earnings call, Zynga reported that they exceeded their top-line bookings forecast by $48 million and adjusted EBITDA forecast by $51 million, driven mainly by the successful launch of FarmVille 2.[42]

We can see that customer-driven innovation through misuse can easily happen on the Internet but how about in the real world? Let's find out.

SOLDIERS

Soldiers are notoriously gifted at bricolage, often having to make do with whatever they have on hand. Unfortunately for soldiers in Iraq, improvised explosive devices (IEDs), which are homemade bombs, were being set up with tripwires to explode when soldiers tripped them by walking into the wires. From March 2003 to July 2009 there were 4326 US troop fatalities in Iraq, many of these from IEDs.[44]

President Bush declared that IEDs 'are now the principal threat to our troops and to the future of a free Iraq'. The United States began pouring billions of dollars and fresh platoons of experts into its campaign to defeat IEDs, but many were skeptical that advanced technology would eliminate the threat. 'As we've improved our armor, the enemy's improved his IEDs. They're bigger, and with better detonating mechanisms', said Major Randall Simmons, whose Georgia National Guard unit escorts convoys in western Iraq that are regularly rocked, damaged, and delayed by roadside blasts. Lt. Col. Bill Adamson, Operations Chief for the anti-IED campaign, was realistic about the challenge in a Pentagon interview: 'They adapt more quickly than we procure technology', he said of the insurgents.[45]

Faced with the escalating use of IEDs in Iraq, the Army Chief of Staff established the Army IED Task Force in October 2003. The task force reached out to all branches of the military service, the private

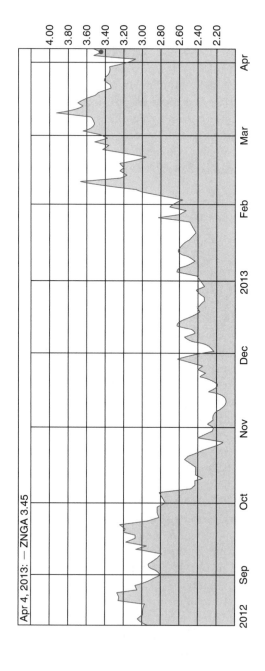

Figure 7.3   *Zynga Stock from 31 Aug 2012 to 8 Apr 2013*[43]

Source: © 2013 Yahoo! Inc.

sector, and academia to acquire counter-IED technologies and develop counter-IED training for US troops. Early success of the Army's task force drove down casualty rates per IED attack, despite an increase in the number of IED incidents. In 2006, Deputy Secretary of Defense, Paul D. Wolfowitz, transformed the Army-led organization into a joint IED task force called the Joint IED Defeat Organization.[46]

While the work by scientists and experts was surely welcomed, soldiers weren't going to sit around and wait for someone else to solve their problems. Lt. Col. Christopher Garver, a US military spokesman in Baghdad, said soldiers and Marines have been encouraged to devise anti-IED methods. The military even went so far as to give commanders money to buy nonstandard supplies.[47] One such nonstandard supply turned out to be Silly String, a toy that is a flexible plastic string, sometimes brightly colored, propelled from an aerosol can. The solvent in the string quickly evaporates in mid-air, creating a continuous strand. Leonard A. Fish and Robert P. Cox patented Silly String in 1972 as a 'foamable resinous composition', originally designed as an aerosol spray cast for limbs. The product was licensed to and produced by Wham-O, a toy company located in California, until the CAR-FRESHNER® Corporation acquired the Silly String trademark in 1997.[48] The CAR-FRESHNER® Corporation manufactured and distributed Silly String under its Watertown, NY division, Just for Kicks, Inc., until 1 January 2013 when they changed the division's name to SILLY STRING Products.[49]

In January 2007, Marcelle Shriver sent several cans of Silly String to her son, Todd, a soldier serving in Ramadi, Iraq. The troops were using it to detect tripwires on bombs. They would shoot the substance, which travels about 10–12 feet, across a room before entering. If the string hangs in the air, it is an indication of a possible tripwire.[50] Eventually Shriver coordinated to have 80,000 cans of the substance shipped to Iraq for soldiers to use in detecting IED tripwires. The manufacturer, Just for Kicks Inc., donated its product to the US military. Rob Oram the Just for Kicks product marketing manager said, 'Everyone in the entire corporation is very pleased that we can be involved in something like this.'[51]

CAR-FRESHNER® Corporation is a private company and therefore we don't have any data on how this impacted sales of the Silly String product. However, a Google search for 'military and silly string' results in over 245,000 hits. In 2007 there was a significant rise in web traffic related to the term 'silly string' (see Figure 7.4, where the number

'100' represents the peak search interest). All of these are indications of more interest in the product that is likely to result in more sales. Enough about bombs and silly string. Let's eat.

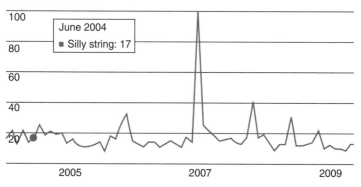

Figure 7.4   *Google Trends for 'Silly String'*

Source: Google and the Google logo are registered trademarks of Google Inc., used with permission.

SUBWAY'S JARED

Born on 1 December 1977, Jared S. Fogle grew up in Indianapolis, Indiana, as a typical Jewish kid, playing outside, riding bikes, and attending summer camps. That is until third grade when he received his first video game, a Nintendo system. He played it for about an hour a day at first, but the amount of time that he spent playing the game grew rapidly until he was spending five or more hours a day on video games. 'It had a huge effect for the negative on my life', said Fogle.[52] Over the years, he exercised less, ate more junk food, and gained weight, ballooning up to more than 425 pounds while in college. He wore pants with a 62-inch waist.

Despite having a physician and teacher for parents – who were concerned over his health – Fogle could not lose the weight. After several failed attempts at losing weight, he got an idea when he saw a sign in his local Subway shop promoting seven sub-sandwiches, each with under 6 grams of fat.[53] 'I was sick and tired of being sick and tired', he said. 'I knew I needed to make some major changes in my life'. His plan was to eat two of the restaurant's low-fat sandwiches each day. Fogle ate a 6-inch turkey sub for lunch and a foot long veggie sub for dinner.

He enjoyed a small bag of baked potato chips with lunch and permitted himself diet soft drinks throughout the day. He skipped breakfast, avoided cheese and mayonnaise on his subs, but loaded his sandwiches with lettuce, green peppers, jalapeno peppers, and pickles. His daily diet totaled less than 10 grams of fat and about 1000 calories.

Bumping into a former college dorm-mate, Ryan Coleman, in April 1999, kicked off a serendipitous chain of events. Coleman barely recognized Fogle because of the amount of weight he had lost – 245 pounds at that point – and decided to write a story about him for the *Indiana Daily Student* newspaper. The editor-in-chief didn't believe the story of someone losing over 200 pounds by eating fast food and almost stopped it from being published.[54] But the article did get published and the story gained steam, eventually being picked up by the Associated Press. *Men's Health* magazine confirmed the story and included the 'Subway sandwich diet' in an article, 'Stupid Diets. . . that Work!'[55]

While some may disagree, we feel that there is a pretty strong argument to be made that Fogle's use of Subway's food was customer misbehavior. Subway's marketing had never before suggested eating only Subway subs as a diet and in fact, until 5 April 2010, Subway did not even sell breakfast foods.[56] Fortunately, a Chicago-area Subway franchisee had the idea that they should take advantage of this misbehavior and suggested it to their advertising agency. The agency confirmed the story by visiting the Subway franchise near the Indiana University campus, where the staff identified Fogle from his description. Another clear indicator that this was viewed as customer misbehavior was that Subway's Marketing Director expressed doubt that as a fast food chain they could successfully market healthfulness of their products and the company's lawyers expressed concerns over liability.[57]

Subway's corporate executives reluctantly agreed to a test in a regional ad campaign, first airing on 1 January 2000. Fogle's story was told along with a disclaimer: 'The Subway diet, combined with a lot of walking, worked for Jared. We're not saying this is for everyone. You should check with your doctor before starting any diet program. But it worked for Jared.'[58]

The commercial was a stunning success, and the day after it aired, Subway's Chicago advertising agency President, Barry Krause, began receiving calls from *USA Today*, *ABC News*, *Fox News*, and *Oprah*. Fogle has become an international celebrity, speaking to thousands of children about fitness and a healthy lifestyle. Over a ten-year period since Fogle's advertising campaign began, Subway sales have more than doubled to $8.2 billion. Of course the amount of gain attributable to Fogle is undeterminable but according to one Subway executive, a brief departure from the Fogle campaign in 2005 coincided with a 10 per cent drop in sales, compelling Subway to bring him back.[59] It is reasonable to attribute a large portion of this 100 per cent gain over ten years to a single customer's misbehavior and the willingness of a Chicago-area Subway franchisee owner to take advantage of it, instead of dismissing it, like the Subway executives and lawyers wanted to do.

CONCLUSION

Some of the most innovative companies understand misuse, misbehavior, or bricolage and actually encourage users to engage in such behavior. Other companies simply are fortunate enough take advantage of misuse without properly identifying it. These companies may or may not get lucky a second or third time. Without a framework to explain and discuss the proper response to customer misbehavior of their product, the company is likely to miss out on great opportunities. Next we will meet some of these companies that missed opportunities. In some cases it helped to destroy their business, in others it was simply a missed opportunity.

Summary

- Coca-Cola and Perfetti Van Melle took advantage of the Eepybird viral video to launch a marketing campaign resulting in increased sales of both products.

- Facebook watched how users misused their 'friend' feature to eventually develop the 'events' feature.

- Twitter's primary purpose was to share moments of people's lives with each other but it has become so much more, impacting on individuals, businesses, and entire governments, largely due to the misuse of the product by users.

- Zynga's FarmVille was a phenomenal success as a social networking game but changes in policies quickly took their toll on this and similar games that relied on sharing across social networks to gain new users. Zynga's designers took note of how users interacted with features in the game such as the livestock and incorporated these changes in FarmVille 2, which has helped bolster the company's stock price.

- Soldiers used a simple toy, 'Silly String', to help save lives by identifying improvised explosive devices that were triggered by tripwires.

- Jared Fogle, an overweight college kid, went on a Subway-only diet and lost over 200 pounds. Reluctant to leverage or hardly even believe this story, Subway almost missed the opportunity. Thanks to the perseverance of a franchisee they launched a decade-long marketing campaign starring Fogle, which helped double sales.

8
Getting it Wrong

eBay, Intuit and Facebook are all shining examples of what happens when a company 'gets it right'. Creating opportunities that allow users to define, validate, and manage their self-identities increases the chances that users will use a company's products and engage in acts of co-creation and co-production. Whether for reasons of identity (as was the case in the Intuit and Facebook examples) or personal utility (as was the case with eBay), by engaging in both co-creation and co-production users are likely to 'misbehave' and use a firm's products in new and unforeseen ways. Each of these uses may represent new value creation opportunities for the firm. The use may extend the ease of use or the usefulness of the product in its current market, as was the case with Intuit's Live Community platform, thereby increasing user satisfaction, retention and overall user account growth. The usage may also open up new addressable markets previously unforeseen by the firm, as was the case with the eBay Motors example. The new usage might also increase the activity level of the current user base, allowing additional opportunities to monetize transactions, as was the case with Facebook.

To successfully capitalize on this opportunity, a firm must both monitor for customer innovation ('misbehavior' or 'bricolage'), fight against the innate tendency of organizations to squelch it, and actively engage in efforts to enable new value-creating activity. Unfortunately, none of this is easy to do. It is very likely that the activity will be so tiny, relative to the primary activity within the product, as to be the veritable 'needle in a haystack'. The opportunity cost of enabling the activity almost always appears to be significant. If a firm beats the odds stacked against it and is lucky enough to find customers innovating on its behalf, it is as likely to kill or disregard the activity as it is to work to enable it. And so what if a firm kills or disregards some emergent user behavior? If the business is successful anyway, shouldn't it just go ahead and continue to do the things it was doing before? Conventional business wisdom – the call for strategic direction – teaches that to be successful, companies need laser-like focus and execution in their target markets, especially when they are young. Isn't this really just a story about lost opportunity? Wouldn't eBay and Intuit still be successful without capitalizing on the low-cost, high-value innovation presented to them by their users?

The answer to these questions for both eBay and Intuit is most likely 'yes'. For both of these companies, the worst thing that was likely to happen was missing an opportunity for shareholder value creation. While this is 'bad' on a relative basis, at least relative to the value they've created by enabling customer innovation, it wasn't a life or death situation for the companies. In the case of eBay, the worst case scenario is likely that another company would have created an efficient selling platform for cars – effectively 'stealing' the opportunity from underneath eBay's nose and limiting their opportunity in that target market. Maybe eBay would have acquired the competing company, or maybe it just would have written off that market. Intuit, on the other hand, may have opened the door for a competitor to create a tax-filing solution with an easier to use interface for solving tax-related questions and in so doing may have lost existing market share to the competitor. At the very least, missing the opportunity created by customer misbehavior invites competition. But our research also uncovered cases where missing or killing customer misbehavior resulted in catastrophic failure for the company. Such was the case with Friendster, often considered the 'father' of modern-day online social networks.

FRIENDSTER – 'THE LOST CIVILIZATION'

'Last month, internet archeologist Dr. Maxwell Frey stumbled upon the perfectly preserved ruins of an online community called Friendster.' So begins the satirical video from 'The Onion', the parody and satire site that proclaims itself to be 'American's Finest News Source'.[1] 'One day', explains the fictitious Dr. Frey, 'Friendster users were posting a seemingly endless stream of bulletins about awesome parties and cool shows and then ... nothing ... Total silence'. Dr. Frey goes on to explain the possible reasons for the 'loss' of the civilization as being an Internet virus, or potentially that Friendster was only meant to be a temporary civilization after the departure of an earlier civilization known as 'Aooohl' (a comedic reference to America Online or AOL, yet another dead Internet civilization).

The real reasons for Friendster's meteoric rise and subsequent cataclysmic fall have nothing to do with Dr. Frey's hypotheses. Both its rise and its fall can be traced back to the factors within the model of viral growth. But before we get into these specifics, let's get deeper into Friendster's history.

Jonathan Abrams founded Friendster in 2002. Jonathan had previously founded Hotlinks in 1998, a bookmark-sharing tool, and before that worked as a software engineer at Netscape and Nortel. In creating Friendster, Jonathan was hoping to create a dating site that wasn't about 'dating'. He imagined a site that would more closely mimic and even improve upon the way in which people interacted in 'the real world',[2] which was by connecting or introducing friends with other friends. Jonathan raised $100,000 from angel investors and started coding the application himself, inviting friends to find bugs as he developed and released the application to the site. Jonathan raised another $300,000 and released Friendster to anyone over the age of 18 in March of 2003. The site allowed users to create profiles that included attributes such as age, relationship status, and geographic location, as well as to post lists of their favorite entertainment activities. To both enable social connectivity and generate user growth, users could invite other friends to join, and in so doing create a link between the profiles (as friends) once an invitee accepted the invitation and the connection or link. Users could write 'testimonials' about each other. While one user could not edit another user's testimonial about her, she could either accept or reject the testimonial outright, thereby determining whether it would be displayed.

Profile pages for a user listed all of that user's connections (or friends) as well as a display of the 'path' between the person viewing the profile and the member whose profile was being viewed. This functionality of Friendster's was called the friend-graph or f-graph. If you were to view Alec Baldwin's page, for instance, the page would display the link of friends that connected you to Alec Baldwin up to four degrees of separation. If there wasn't a linkage within four degrees, you wouldn't be able to see Alec. This limitation was lifted roughly a year after launch, allowing anyone to see anyone else's profile page unless a member restricted access to either friends, or friends of friends.[3] To visualize this path, think of it as being similar to the popular parlor game 'Six Degrees of Kevin Bacon' built around the assumption that any two people on earth are on average only 'six degrees apart'. The game asks players to connect some arbitrary actor to Kevin Bacon through other actors with which he has worked in no more than a total of six steps or films.

The initial Friendster product was, by any measure, an absolute success. Without any marketing, Friendster's viral growth achieved one million users within the first four months of launch![4] Abrams and/or Friendster received coverage in the *Wall Street Journal, Newsweek, Esquire,* and *Vanity Fair* and on CNN.[5] He was named a Breakout Star by *Entertainment Weekly* and was on *Jimmy Kimmel Live* – something even the founders of Yahoo had not achieved.[6] Google took notice of the success of Friendster and offered to acquire the rather young company for the then princely sum of $30 million. But Abrams, who reportedly would show up at Silicon Valley parties with a beautiful woman on each arm,[7] had even greater ambitions for Friendster. Legendary Silicon Valley venture capital firms such as Benchmark and Kleiner Perkins chased after Friendster and urged Abrams to spurn Google's overtures and instead 'go big'. Abrams accepted both the challenge and the money of the venture capitalists and with $13 million in new venture capital funding and a $53 million valuation for Friendster, set out to prove the forecast of the *Venture Capital Journal* that 'the Net is hot again'.[8]

ELEMENTS OF SUCCESS

Friendster's story so far is one of incredible success. It was so successful in fact that (in hindsight) *Inc. Magazine* called it one of the greatest successes up to the point of the venture capital funding and since the 'dot com' bust.[9] While this chapter is about failure, it's valuable to take just a moment to dissect the reasons for the success of Friendster. Clearly, as the one million active users in four months indicate, the product achieved a viral coefficient greater than 1.0 and as a result achieved viral success. In explaining this success we can use many elements of our model.

Friendster's initial product played to the identity definition and self-verification of users (Chapters 4–6). Users could post content and information about themselves as well as describe their favorite things – all elements of identification theory as described in Chapter 6. Additionally, through the notion of testimonials, users could provide feedback about other people, which in turn allows those people to 'verify' who they are. Even Abrams, as recognized by *Inc. Magazine*, felt that he had created something meaningful to identity – 'a piece of software that could tell us who we were'.[10] Users could 'disregard' the information and have it discarded if it didn't meet their individual beliefs about themselves. Recall from Chapter 5 that people seek validation of their beliefs, so the features that we build should enforce this need for verification. Allowing users to disregard testimonials inconsistent with their beliefs supports this need for validation. These features clearly all enable the element of *identity*, including *voyeurism*, *exhibitionism*, and *self-verification*. Identity – check!

Users were also involved in *co-creating* content with Friendster. Recall that *co-creation* is the act of firms and users engaging together to create content for user consumption. Allowed to post information about themselves, create lists, and comment on other users through testimonials, the users were co-creating with Friendster. Also recall that enabling co-creation is a critical action we recommend that firms pursue within their products (see Chapter 3) to help enable viral growth. Co-creation – check!

While it's hard to objectively evaluate the *usefulness* and *ease of use* of the site, given that it no longer exists as it did in 2003, we think it is fair to say that users felt it was both useful and easy to use. How else could something achieve such phenomenal growth, attract the attention of such institutionally wise and knowledgeable investors, and achieve such critical acclaim at the time? Furthermore, as we will see in just a few minutes, something changed along both of these dimensions that further indicates that the product was *useful* and *easy to use*. Useful and easy to use – check!

Moreover despite Abrams' initial vision of the site as an improvement on dating, users seemed to be using it to keep up with friends, and friends of friends.[11] Users were using the site in an unexpected way! They had taken the site, used it for a new need (*co-production*) and this new and unforeseen use was embraced by Friendster and was driving the success! Co-production – check!

OK – so identity and usefulness lead to a virtuous cycle of co-creation and co-production. In conjunction with ease of use we appear to have *fan-out* and *retention* and therefore *viral growth*. All systems are go! We have launch! But wait a minute Houston – we are about to have a problem.

WHAT GOES UP MUST COME DOWN

The 'Black Hats', or enlisted instructors, at the US Army Airborne School in Ft. Benning, GA, used to have a saying that they would repeat to every new class of paratroopers. 'Don't be afraid to fall', the instructors would say. 'It's not the fall that will kill you, it's the sudden stop!' The implied idea here is that, as long as you did what you were taught, there was nothing to fear from a fall itself. You simply needed to recognize that you were in a fall, ensure that you took the appropriate actions, and you would land safely on the ground. But when things started going wrong at Friendster, it appears that they neither accepted that they were falling nor took the appropriate steps to stop the fall. Moreover sometimes they appeared to take actions that would accelerate the decline by providing new opportunities to new competitors.

The first manifestation of problems for Friendster occurred with the performance of the site. By late 2003, users were complaining that pages were not only taking a long time to load, but were often incomplete as well.[12] It's important to remember that there were several factors at work here. The first is that the site was experiencing seldom-witnessed exponential growth. In many weeks, membership on the site was growing at an astonishing 25 per cent per week.[13] This was also late 2003, and 'the Cloud' (or Infrastructure as a Service – IaaS, as technologists call it) had not yet been invented. Every time Friendster wanted a new server to add capacity to the site to serve requests, they needed to either purchase it or request it from their services provider. The server would need to be racked, installed, powered up and configured with the appropriate software to run the service. The entire procedure could take days, and indeed for many companies could sometimes take weeks. Today with IaaS cloud-providers such as Amazon and Rackspac, this can often be done in minutes. If Friendster didn't accurately predict the demand for their services well in advance (and they didn't) and order the servers to be ready, they wouldn't be able to serve the entire onslaught of traffic brought on by viral user acquisition.

Under the covers, there was even more going on from a technology perspective. Even when Friendster brought in additional servers, page load times still couldn't be reduced to satisfactory times. Initially, engineers blamed the way that the new and more expensive servers were configured,[14] but through several rounds of changes in server configuration, load times were still staggeringly slow. Not only had Abrams and his team never planned for the servers necessary to serve such a deluge of traffic, they hadn't really thought about the memory, disc, database, and CPU limitations of the systems serving that traffic. As Friendster's total user base grew, the cost and time to calculate the friend-graph (every connection of every friend), and to display the results on a page, grew as well. Remember that for every profile page served, the person viewing that page would see the f-graph of connections from the viewer to the member's profile page. It turns out that the method of performing this calculation in real time was expensive in both CPU cycles and total processing time. As long as the user base continued to increase in size, the problem was going to get harder and page load times slower.

Sites that experience rapid or viral growth often experience situations similar to Friendster's.[15] It is common for engineers to develop sites rapidly with the notion of the site working on a handful of servers and serving a small number of users without anticipating what will happen when database servers end up having to compute relationships across ever-increasing user bases.[16] When rapid growth comes, faster and larger systems simply can't keep up with the increase in demand and the product needs to be redesigned. Many successful sites, including eBay, ultimately experienced similar problems and had to rejigger their solutions in order to solve the increase in user demand.[17] Sometimes it means shutting off certain features so that servers have the capacity for more critical features to function, as eBay did with the 'myeBay' feature in 1999.[18]

It's important to note here that, at this point in Friendster's history, they are starting to experience trouble with our model of viral growth. Page load times are clearly critical and when load times increase, the *usefulness* of the service decreases accordingly.[19] Our model predicts that a reduction of usefulness will then negatively affect fan-out and retention, and therefore viral growth. Furthermore a reduction in usefulness will negatively affect the virtuous cycle of customer misbehavior. The good news is that Friendster, at this point in their story, still has some time to fix things. eBay successfully navigated its technology failures in 1999 to become and remain a major player in online commerce.[20] In fact, most successful Internet businesses have had significant problems from time to time.[21] But to be successful, they ultimately must be solved quickly. Let's put a bookmark in our story about page load times so that we can switch to another Friendster story that has implications for our model of viral growth.

FRIENDSTER AND THE LEAD USER PROBLEM

Early users started to use Friendster for unforeseen uses as predicted by our model – for example, as a product to keep track of friends, rather than to find dates through friends. They started to do something else very new and innovative. Friendster employees coined two terms for these customer misbehaviors: Fakesters and Fraudsters. Fakesters were users who set up profile pages to identify religious, mythical, or fictitious characters. Profile pages for God, Hippy Jesus, Homer Simpson, and Cartman from South Park started to appear on the site. Other Fakester pages might include groups of people, events, food and drink, or sports teams such as 'Knights of Columbus', 'Gay Pride Parade', 'Beer', or 'San Francisco 49ers'.[22] Fraudsters, while similar in that they represented something other than the creator of the profile page, were different in that they either represented real people who had yet to join Friendster (such as celebrities or friends) or simply weren't people or characters at all. Neither of these types of profiles were 'real' in the sense of identifying the person who set up the profile and, as such, they were inconsistent with the intended purpose of Friendster.

Here we have good examples of the good and bad misbehavior we discussed in Chapter 3. Fakesters appear to be something that firms would want to enable, and Fraudsters something they may want to monitor closely or disable. Fraudsters may have an element of identity theft or other mischievous behavior. We know from the stories in Chapter 7 and our model that, at least with respect to Fakesters, Friendster had just struck a gold mine! But did Abrams enable this misbehavior? No! 'Fake profiles really defeats [sic] the whole point of Friendster', said Abrams. 'Some people find it amusing, but some find it annoying. And it doesn't really serve a legitimate purpose. The whole point of Friendster is to see how you're connected to people through your friends.'[23]

Even *Salon* magazine seemed to hit on something important here. As quoted from their article: 'But some of Friendster's members maintain that the site is so popular because of the created and unexpected ways its early inhabitants used it.'[24] Abrams didn't agree, arguing 'that it's really just a small percentage of the overall users who create or make friends with fakesters'.[25] And just like that, Abrams fell prey to one of the pitfalls we identified in Chapter 3 – the underestimation of a potential market for newly-identified customer misbehavior. The company began to remove fake profiles as some users complained about them. Both *Salon* and *Wired Magazine* referred to Friendster's actions as the 'Fakester Genocide'.

Users revolted in various ways. One well-known and well-liked Fakester, 'Giant Squid', wrote on his 'about me' page before being suspended, 'What kind of person creates a revenue model that involves the deliberate exclusion of potential customers?'[26] One former Fakester created the website 'Dogster' for the display of dogs, as they were also not allowed under the Fakester policy. Fraudsters started to put up 'Johnny Clone' profiles that would pretend to be Jonathan Abrams with funny statements in their 'about me' pages. One such profile stated, 'I'm a <expletive> wanker who has such a hard time meeting women that I invented my own dating service. For some reason, no one used it for that purpose though.'[27] In a small gesture to the Fakester community, Abrams and team did allow the Dreamworks movie *Anchorman* to display fictitious characters on its site, but such actions were rare.[28]

Now in relation to our model of viral growth, Friendster has another problem. Instead of enabling the virtuous cycle of customer misbehavior, Friendster acted as most companies do and squashed it. If Friendster had a burgeoning problem on its hands before, the problem has now escalated into one the size of Apollo 13. But hold on, a new team is on its way to help out!

THE REVOLVING DOOR OF HELP

In defense of Friendster, both the Board and the management team recognized and started to act upon the page performance problems. They hired a new VP of Engineering and set a deadline of April 2004 to have a completely overhauled and properly functioning (including faster page performance) site deployed. The company had plenty of funding from their new investment and began to hire 'the best of the best' from other companies like Netscape, Yahoo, Google, Amazon, and eBay – companies that had experienced similar growth before and prevailed over the problems that growth exposed. The augmented engineering team, while comprised of stellar individuals, was not yet cohesive and as a result couldn't agree on what to do.[29] The original date of April was clearly going to be missed, the old plan of overhauling the Java code by April 2004 was scrapped, and a new plan of rewriting the application in PHP was hatched. Half of Friendster's engineers were deployed against this new plan, but the new PHP instances of the site were 'buggy' and increased the level of aggravation of already annoyed users.[30]

In addition to the new VP of Engineering, Friendster hired a VP of Product Management from Yahoo and an interim CEO, Tim Koogle, also formerly of Yahoo. Abrams was removed from the CEO position but retained his Chairman title. With the engineering team nearly fully deployed against launching a new site in PHP, or fixing the current Java version, there was little extra time for new features. Conflicts started to develop along the organizational boundary between the product management team and the engineering team. An HR manager from Friendster recalled product managers saying, 'I just want it done, I don't care how you do it'. To which an engineer replied, 'I can't do it this way and you don't value my opinion.'[31]

By June 2004, interim CEO Tim Koogle was replaced by Scott Sassa. Scott was an experienced executive from the media industry, having been the President of both NBC Entertainment and NBC West Coast. The level of conflict between organization and executives was 'like a War in Valhalla' with each executive seeming to have their own agenda.[32] Scott made a change in the head of engineering at the end of 2004, and invited an additional Director, Jeff Katz (founding CEO and Chairman of Orbitz) onto the Board. Katz helped to spearhead a 90-day strategy assessment to identify what users wanted in a social networking platform.[33] While the assessment was timely, with Myspace having just passed Friendster in reach, users, and page views, the strategies presented to the Board did not include addressing the elimination of Fakesters. And why would they? Consistent with Von Hippel's analysis at 3M, companies simply don't see lead user behavior (or customer misbehavior) as significant enough to act upon. Sassa left Friendster roughly a year into the job, in mid-2005, but not before the company found out that a significant portion of their traffic was coming from the Philippines.

The Philippines discovery was the harbinger of the last phase of Friendster's short honeymoon period with success. The company identified that a significant spike in traffic was occurring at 2 a.m. in the morning. Through log analysis, Friendster saw that much of the traffic was coming from the Philippines. The 91st user of Friendster had befriended a dozen Filipinos and the product took off like wildfire from there in the Philippines and continued to grow through the tech crises, even while US growth dwindled and ultimately fell.[34] This discovery was hailed as a disaster internally as the company was spending a great deal of money to attract 'eyeballs' in the United States and all of the growth was outside of the United States! More than half of the site's traffic was coming from Southeast Asia alone.[35]

THE CHANGING COMPETITIVE LANDSCAPE AND FINALLY A SALE!

While Friendster attempted to deal with its technology problems, determine what to do with 'The Asian Discovery', and suffer through internal conflict, competitors around them were redefining what social networking meant. Friendster's decision to close the door on Fakesters stood in sharp contrast to Facebook's decision (Chapter 7) to embrace and enable the usage. While Friendster kicked off users with profile pages for their universities, teams, interests, and pets, Facebook enabled such usage through group pages, class pages, and applications such as Dogbook and Catbook. Myspace, which allowed anyone to look at anyone else's pictures and hadn't adopted the difficult problem of calculating network graphs (one of the primary causes of Friendster's problems and the cause of slow page downloads) was also rocketing past Friendster. By the end of 2004, Myspace had surpassed Friendster in total users and by mid-to-late 2005 it had 22 million unique users per month, compared to 1.1 million for Friendster.[36] People, it seemed, just wanted to manage their identities, gawk at other users, and generally be voyeuristic and exhibitionist. They wanted to create pages that displayed their interest in political parties, classes at university, bands, sports teams, and pets – not to be pejoratively termed Fakesters.

The writing was on the wall for Friendster. More CEOs came and went, employees departed as they became demoralized with the success of Facebook and Myspace. Friendster made the Asian market, where it dominated, a priority. On 9 December 2009 it was acquired by MOL, a Malaysian company, for $26.4 million.

MEANWHILE IN THE 'REAL WORLD'

Most of the references within this book have been of Internet sensations the likes of Intuit, eBay, Facebook, and Friendster. Here and there we've made references to 'traditional' companies like 3M and Tupperware. Lest one starts to believe that 'getting it wrong' can only happen in the world of the Internet, here's a quick story of how one very successful company got at least one small thing very wrong.

Jose Avila, a software developer, was locked into two rents after moving to Arizona from California, and had no extra cash for even an Ikea futon. Instead of hunting for used, stained couches and bedding, in a classic case of 'misuse', he built an apartment full of furniture out of FedEx shipping boxes. He also put up a site, fedexfurniture.com, to share his creativity. His furniture creations include a bed, a corner desk with shelves, a table, two chairs, and a couch. The designs are surprisingly un-boxy and sturdy.[37]

FedEx however were not amused, and on 27 June 2005, three days after the site went live, they sent Avila a cease-and-desist letter demanding he take down the site, citing among other things the Digital Millennium Copyright Act. Avila claimed that he was blindsided by the cease-and-desist letter from the company to which he proclaims long-standing loyalty. 'I was surprised', Avila said. 'One thing I've always stood behind is I'm pro-FedEx. I ship stuff with FedEx all the time and I feel more comfortable shipping with FedEx because their boxes are stable and sturdy.'[38]

While the impact on FedEx's business is likely small monetarily, they nonetheless did receive some terrible press even from people such as Seth Godin, who stated in his blog, 'This site featuring cheesy furniture (FedexFurniture.Com) would have essentially no traffic – except for the fact that Fedex sent a cease-and-desist letter and claimed it violated the DCMA[sic] ... No, it probably won't hurt Fedex's business, but it's sure not worth the hassle, is it?'

Another individual, Michael Gray, wrote a post on threadwatch.org: 'Fedex Furniture & How to be a Corporate Wanker', in which he pondered, 'To really think out of the box (pardon the pun) why not run a contest every year and invite people to build stuff out of the boxes. Think of how many news stations would do a 60 second spot about it.'

FedEx reacted poorly to their product misuse. This cost the company popular opinion as well as resources to pursue this. Fortunately FedEx has not made a pattern of ignoring customers and in fact has been incredibly innovative with regard to the demands of customers. They have a dedicated cross-discipline team, FedEx Innovation, which is focused on 'identifying emerging customer needs and technologies to change what's possible'.[39] Even great companies like Apple and FedEx need to rely on customers' usage and misuse in order to know truly what customers want.

CONCLUSION

Models can be useful when they help demonstrate how you can achieve success. Their value increases when they can help explain how and why things went poorly. The Friendster story outlined in this chapter helps show how our model of viral growth can help not only propel companies to viral success, but save them from vicious disaster.

Friendster started out doing everything properly. They enabled users to define and self-verify their identities. They created a system that, as long as it wasn't overloaded, was easy to use and perceived useful by its users. While they initially desired to create a site that would help reinvent and improve upon the dating experience, they identified that users were using it for something they had not expected and they enabled that usage. Each piece of our model received a 'check box' and viral growth ensued. Friendster became an Internet and media darling.

But then things turned badly for every piece of our model. Technology problems in computing the friend-graph that displayed the distance between users for each view of any profile page caused slow page loads. User experience vis-à-vis both perceived usefulness and perceived ease of use was impaired. While the company intended to fix these issues, infighting and bickering between groups helped to delay fixes and further aggravate users.

Friendster also stopped users from creating what they called 'Fakester' accounts. These accounts consisted of profiles for their pets, profiles for favorite fictional characters, and the equivalent of the successful 'groups' features on Facebook. Whereas Friendster had initially enabled customer misbehavior to become successful, they now deemed this emergent customer misbehavior as both a threat to their platform and too small to enable. The 'Fakester Genocide' helped drive users to create new platforms and exit Friendster for competing products like Myspace and Facebook.

Finally, Friendster didn't notice through the smoke of their problems and infighting that the competitive landscape had changed. Competitors were moving to enable new behaviors around identity – that of exhibitionism and voyeurism. While concerns over privacy have since moved competition away from the lax standards prevalent in 2005, there is no doubt in our minds that this emergent customer behavior helped propel Friendster's competitors past them in terms of page views, unique users, and reach.

While we have seen a lot of examples, both good and bad, of how Internet-based companies react to customer misbehavior, it is not exclusive to online businesses. As we saw with FedEx, even large, brick and mortar companies who recognize the power of customer innovation can falter and shut down potential benefits by labeling the use as misuse.

Our model in no way indicates that a company that fails to promote viral growth through the creation of an easy to use and useful product, the enablement of identity, and active co-production with their users will fail. The model only indicates that it is much more difficult to achieve viral growth in the absence of all of these things. However there are certain industries in which there appears to be a 'winner take all' or 'natural monopoly' – where it is better to have a single product or service to serve everyone's needs, rather than multiple products or services. These industries seem to be characterized by 'network effects', where more supply (sellers or question answerers) begets more demand (buyers and question askers) and where the entire value to everyone increases as a result. Social networks appear to be one such case, where people have only so much time, so they will engage in the network that has the highest total value in terms of friends and content. In cases like these, it is entirely possible that the model can be used to predict both success and failure, as is the case with the stark contrast between Facebook and Friendster.

Summary

- The concepts of identity, co-creation, co-production, ease of use, and usefulness serve not only as a guidepost for success, but as warnings of potential failure. Seek to set up processes that help identify when you are doing things to limit any of them.

- Just as encouraging any of these concepts can aid you in achieving viral growth; discouraging or even ignoring these concepts can chart a path to failure.

- Guard against the common practice of under-appreciating emergent customer behavior. Be careful of pejorative terms when you identify it. Choose to enable it and succeed, rather than disable it and fail.

9
Conclusion

We've spent a great deal of time discussing viral concepts within the context of consumer-based (business-to-consumer or B2C) businesses. This focus on consumer-based companies, coupled with the concept of fan-out within the viral growth equation itself, may even lead one to believe that viral growth is only feasible within consumer-oriented businesses. The notion within fan-out of referring others to a product just seems, at least to the authors, to be something that people do with products they use in their everyday lives – not something businesses do between each other. Our experience as practitioners is that companies are 'sold' products by legions of sales people, who are in turn employed for their skills in persuading companies to buy products. Companies purchasing products typically implement processes to request proposals ('RFPs') from product-producing companies in order to more objectively evaluate feature sets, price points, and suitability of the competing products to fit their needs. The sales cycle for technology products is often a long and onerous one, taking from several weeks to over a year. Implementation of the products can take even longer, with multiple teams gearing up to identify how to modify the product to meet internal business needs. Careers can hang in the balance as multi-million dollar implementations of complex systems take months and even years to complete. This 'friction' within the sales and implementation cycle seems to indicate that viral growth simply doesn't happen and indeed isn't possible within business-to-business (B2B) models. Or is it?

Marc Benioff grew up in the San Francisco metropolitan area. An entrepreneur from an early age, Marc founded Liberty Software while in high school, to create and sell games for the Atari system. During the summer of 1984, between semesters working towards a degree in business administration from the University of Southern California, Benioff took a job as an assembly language programmer in Apple's Macintosh division. That summer, while working under a pirate flag hoisted over the Macintosh staff building by the legendary Steve Jobs, Benioff 'discovered it was possible for an entrepreneur to encourage revolutionary ideas'.[1] After completing his degree, Benioff went to work for Oracle where he was named 'Rookie of the Year' and rose to the rank of VP in only three years. Benioff would go on to spend 13 years at Oracle and while working there invest in a customer relationship management (CRM) software startup, Siebel Software, founded by one of his former Oracle colleagues, Tom Siebel. As if presaged by the flag flying over the Macintosh building in 1984, Benioff would sell his stake in Siebel and use the funds to found a company focusing on disruptive innovation within the CRM space. Together with software developers Parker Harris, Dave Moellenhoff, and Frank Dominguez, Benioff founded Salesforce.com Inc. in March 1999.

The disruptive element of Benioff and his team's approach was to deliver and sell CRM software 'as a service', rather than as a package that a customer would install at their site or 'on premise' as it is known in the industry. Selling Software-as-a-Service (SaaS) meant that the software would be hosted and operated by Salesforce.com, accessed over the Internet by a customer, and paid for via subscription rather than the traditional software license model. The new business model traded large, upfront, one-time license fees for a recurring revenue model paid monthly, quarterly, or annually. Within four years the company had acquired 8700 customers (companies with a contract to use the Salesforce.com service) with 127,000 subscribers (employees of the companies purchasing the service who were actually using the Salesforce.com product – sometimes referred to as 'seats'). In June 2004, the company raised $110 million in their initial public offering (IPO) on the New York Stock Exchange. By the end of 2007, Salesforce.com had over 38,000 customers and one million subscribers. To achieve this growth from 127,000 subscribers in June 2004 to one million subscribers in 2007, the company needed to roughly double its subscriber base per annum, resulting in a growth chart similar to that of Figure 9.1.

While not completely 'viral' in practice, as we've described in the viral growth equation, resulting solely from word of mouth fan-out of the product from interested users, Salesforce.com's growth was nevertheless viral in its resulting subscription numbers. The very nature of their growth, as the line in Figure 9.1 displays, indicates an exponential growth, year over year, relative to the starting numbers in 2004. Recall that viral growth typically results in an S-curve, with the early effects of such growth resulting in a steep incline of total users over

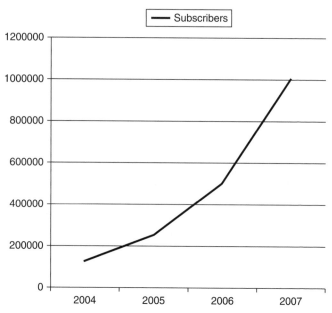

Figure 9.1 *Salesforce.com Subscriber Growth*

time and a declining increase of users as the market nears full penetration. Figure 9.1 above shows such an early beginning to an S-curve.

It would be difficult to argue that Salesforce.com's growth was completely or even mostly a result of word of mouth referrals to their product. Practitioners understand that companies simply do not operate the same way that an individual consumer may when considering product purchases. While companies definitely refer products to each other, they are much more likely to engage in processes that slow the speed with which any given product may be acquired.[2] Adoption, then, tends to be less about the referral or act of fan-out itself than a purposeful effort of product evaluation to fit specific needs. As such, we won't claim that fan-out (at least as we described it in Chapter 1) is a good way to describe Salesforce.com's growth, but there are other elements of our model at play that helped them achieve these astounding results.

Recall that concepts borrowed from the Technology Acceptance Model are critical to our explanation of viral growth. Specifically within our model, the Technology Acceptance Model constructs *ease of use* and *usefulness* are both highly correlated with viral growth. Salesforce.com offered a solution enabled as a service that allowed companies to bypass the cumbersome and costly process of implementing software at a customer's site or 'on premise'. In so doing, they provided a solution that was easier to implement and hence easier to use than the alternatives on the market such as Siebel. Companies could purchase a handful or a large number of 'seats' and allow employees to use them almost immediately (*ease of use*) and gain value from the insights and functionality that the seats enabled (*useful*). Also recall that ease of use is related to usefulness in that products that are easier to use are also generally viewed to be more useful by customers.

Let's jump back into our story of Salesforce.com. By 2005, revenues at Salesforce.com were growing at more than 80 per cent annually, with net income growing even faster. But as was the case with so many other successful companies in our research, the vital software development function that was the heart of Salesforce.com was starting to show signs of strain, brought on by the heady weight of viral success.

The pace of releases of new software features slowed from four times per year to once per year and morale was suffering. Almost back-to-back in late 2005, the company experienced an infrastructure failure that caused a major service interruption for customers, and a highly respected senior developer gave a scathing offsite presentation criticizing the current situation and then quit. Another service interruption occurred in early 2006, further eroding both the morale of the internal software developers and the overall satisfaction of customers.[3]

However, Salesforce.com had built a base of fanatical customers by focusing on small-to-medium size businesses that were underserved by the traditional enterprise software companies. As Hilarie Koplow-McAdams, President of Commercial & Small Business, stated at the 2012 Dreamforce conference, 'the cloud is democratic', meaning that even the smallest company can now own the same CRM software that the giants in the industry owned, another sign of the usefulness of the product to an underserved market segment.[4] This fanatical user base self-organized itself into user groups that at the time were commonly organized by larger enterprise companies for their customers. These groups gave enterprise customers the opportunity to share knowledge, attend conferences, and interface with the software company's executives.

By 2013 there were over 90 self-managed Salesforce.com user groups. These groups and the companies they represented proved to be an especially fertile source of innovation. Salesforce.com's CRM was both low-cost and highly customizable by the average user. As the platform evolved, it became increasingly customizable, which encouraged more users to customize it and share those customizations. In 2013, Salesforce.com was ranked as the most innovative company in America by *Forbes* magazine.[5]

One of those innovations was the Salesforce.com AppExchange, launched in 2006 as a cloud-computing marketplace, developed and hosted by Salesforce.com. This marketplace was launched before Apple's App Store or Google's Apps Marketplace. For developers, AppExchange is a community where they can build, develop, customize, and market applications or customizations. The application development is done through a Platform as a Service (PaaS) solution named Force.com. PaaS solutions provide development platforms (languages, infrastructure, runtime environments, and so on) over the Internet, meaning that just as with SaaS solutions there is no need to install the software – everything is done through a hosted interface. Developers contributing to the AppExchange get to choose whether they want to charge for their applications or give them away for free.

For customers and users, AppExchange allows access to thousands of applications built by Salesforce.com as well as other developers. AppExchange allows people across different business functions – such as Human Resources, IT, sourcing, and finance – to access numerous applications in a wide variety of categories, such as reporting, staffing, recruiting, and sales. By October 2011, a scant five years after the launch of the platform, the AppExchange had reached the incredible milestone of one million downloads. As one Salesforce.com user put it, 'I have taken applications off the AppExchange, downloaded them to my sandbox, and have customized and made it totally unrecognizable from what it was when I first downloaded it, so that it would fit exactly what my business needed.'[6] And here we see another aspect of our model of viral growth – the enablement of *co-creation* and *co-production* within the Salesforce.com service offering. Salesforce.com seemingly leapt past the need to identify customer misbehavior and instead simply erected a playground in which they could misbehave and *co-produce* to their hearts desire! Furthermore, they created an easy to use interface to allow users to co-produce while incenting co-production through revenue-sharing of the co-produced applications sold in the AppExchange. After all, what is more useful than money?

Salesforce.com is somewhat unique within our research in that the company purposefully built a way for customers to co-produce. In purposefully building co-production into their product, they apparently sidestepped the far too often defining moment in a company's history of identifying customer misuse and then struggling with how to handle it. Whereas so many companies fall back on processes that favor internal innovation and either discard as not valuable, or worse disable, customer innovation, Salesforce.com built a process to embrace and enable it. In innovating and helping to define a new type of business, SaaS, by delivering a service rather than software, Salesforce.com created an *easier to use* and therefore even more *useful* product.

Some products gain viral adoption solely through their ease of use and usefulness. Others seem to have very little utility, but allow for a great deal of 'infotainment', identity resolution and verification. With Salesforce.com there is a degree of both. Not only does the App Exchange provide useful and easy-to-use extensions and add-ons, it also allows developers a central place to showcase their skills and wares. Each application in the exchange gets a 'Provider' tab, dedicated to the developer or company. This can include the developer's website, email, phone number, a brief description, and of course other applications that they have developed. As the sponsoring company or developer gets to decide whether to charge or not for the application, the motivation is likely to differ greatly between larger companies that develop and sell applications and individual software engineers who build applications for free.

Where compensation is not involved (that is, the developer offers the solution for 'free'), developer incentives to contribute can be likened to the incentives for contributing to open source projects. The reasons for open source software contribution has been widely studied and appears to be similar to that of social movements such as the civil rights movement, the labor movement, or the peace movement, which includes the identification with that group and hedonistic motives such as enjoyment or reputation.[7] This expression and reinforcement of one's self-identity fits another cog in our model. However not nearly all Salesforce.com subscribers are software developers. In fact the ease of use of the product ensures this is not necessarily the case. Recognizing that identity is valuable but not absolutely necessary to viral growth, wouldn't Salesforce.com be better off by allowing non-development minded Salesforce.com subscribers to also demonstrate and validate their self-identity?

Salesforce.com seems to believe, as do we, that the answer is 'yes'. On 18 November 2009, Salesforce.com announced 'Salesforce Chatter' – where 'Enterprise Collaboration Meets the Real Time Social Computing Model Loved by Millions on Facebook and Twitter'.[8] Chatter is a real-time collaboration platform for Salesforce.com users.

Similar to Facebook's news feed, the Chatter service sends information in real time proactively. Subscribers can follow co-workers, receive updates about projects, and be kept informed of a customer's status. Users can also form groups and post messages on each other's profiles to collaborate on projects. All of which provides a mechanism that is not only easy to use and useful, but also an avenue for displaying one's self-identity. Project managers can display their knowledge, expertise, and wit by posting clever and frequent updates. Customer service reps can display their dedication by posting updates off-hours. Marc Benioff believes so passionately about this method of collaboration that he declared Chatter as the primary communications interface for all of Salesforce.com.[9]

THE YOUTUBE STORY

We would feel as though we had let some very good friends down if we didn't include at least one great success story from some former employees of ours. As Maryrose Dunton, the Director of Product Development and one of the first product managers at YouTube, recalls, 'YouTube was initially a technology looking for a business problem to solve.' The founders experimented with various practical implementations of their technology, which allowed one to upload and share videos in a 'flash' player. They thought the technology and the site might be used to showcase real estate for sale or used as a dating site to give personal testimonials. 'But instead', said Maryrose, 'we found that people were uploading videos of their cats and of them performing skateboarding tricks. We thought "Really? That's how they want to use it?" We took their lead and came up with the moniker "Broadcast Yourself" – something that still exists today.'

This first example is a great one that displays not only how customers define their identity online and come up with innovative ways to use and even misuse a product, but also how a company can enable that misuse for its own benefit. As Maryrose's incredulous question shows ('Really? That's how they want to use it?'), the team was not expecting people to post funny animal tricks and silly videos of themselves online. They could very well have shut down such usage right then. But instead the team enabled the usage and even created a marketing tagline based on it.

The team at YouTube could hardly be called one-hit wonders. As Maryrose relates the story, the team early on identified users cutting and pasting the URLs associated with videos into their websites, blogs, and Myspace pages. While such usage wasn't really achieving the desired goals of attracting and retaining viewers for long periods of time, in order to advertise to them, nonetheless the team 'bit the bullet' and decided to help enable the usage. The engineering team created an embedded video player that could be placed within any web page. Users could now simply hit 'play', rather than clicking through to another site. Voila! Usage took off and soon 25 per cent of the total videos played on YouTube were done so off the YouTube site via the embedded video player.

What makes this story so interesting is that the off-site, embedded video players were extremely difficult to monetize. At the time, YouTube had no way to insert ads into these videos and the only homage to the YouTube brand was a small watermark within the video player itself, displaying the YouTube logo. But fan-out was incredible and ultimately the team identified how to promote other videos within the player and bring users back to the YouTube site.

The result of YouTube's successful enablement of customer misuse was an acquisition by Google via an all-stock deal valued at $1.65 billion in October 2006.[10] While that seems to be a lofty valuation for a site that reportedly generated only $15 million in revenue in 2006 at the time of acquisition,[11] analysts now believe that YouTube may produce as much as $3.6 billion in revenue as of the year 2012.[12]

MODEL REVIEW

While we've tried to bring our model to life through the case studies of several companies, it is sometimes easy to 'not see the forest for the trees' and lose track of the bigger picture. Let's wrap up by reviewing the major concepts within our model followed by a list of practical suggestions for implementing them within the products that a company may produce.

Growth in for-profit firms is valuable as it engenders greater returns to the stakeholders of the firm. Viral growth is the 'king' of growth as it follows an exponential curve initially, accelerating until market saturation or near complete adoption is achieved, at which point it tapers off and finally levels out. The result of such growth is an S-curve when plotted with consumers on the Y-axis and time on the X-axis of a graph. Viral growth is often achieved when any user, on average, results in more than one additional user being activated and 'retained' on the product through the action of recommending or 'sharing' the product. The result of this process is known as the viral coefficient (C_v) as defined and illustrated in math in Chapter 1. We also noted that achieving true viral growth, where the viral coefficient was greater than one ($C_v > 1$), was very rare and in fact impossible over an infinite time period as sooner or later the product reaches complete market adoption (hence the 'S'-shaped curve). However this doesn't mean that we can't use organic growth (at less than viral levels) to augment our marketing efforts.

Recall that *ease of use* and *usefulness* – concepts borrowed from the Technology Acceptance Model – are highly correlated with viral growth. The easier that a product is to use, the higher the growth in usage of that product and the more users are likely to view that product as useful. Additionally the more useful a product is (driven by both ease of use and the perceived product utility), the higher the likelihood of growth (as indicated by fan-out and retention).

Usefulness also seems to drive a virtuous cycle of co-creation and co-production within products with these latter concepts also being highly correlated with fan-out and retention. The more useful a product, the more likely users will co-create or contribute to content and utility of the product. The more users help co-create a product, the more they are likely to co-produce the product. Recall that co-production is the act of users using a product in new and previously unimagined ways that ultimately either extend the utility of the product within an existing market segment or help to extend the product to new market segments.

Recall that co-production most often occurs initially in small and difficult to recognize clusters of activity shielded by the larger expected activities within a given product. Companies must first either stumble across the unexpected activity or implement processes to specifically mine for and identify such activities within their products. Once found, companies must then fight against the tendency to discount the value of the activity or fight to squelch it as being inconsistent with the firm's desired product and user behavior. Together, co-creation and co-production create a virtuous cycle of low-cost innovation for the firm, if the employees are lucky enough or focused enough to harness it.

The concept of self-identity is highly correlated with the virtuous cycle of co-creation and co-production. Products that enable self-identity definition or verification are highly correlated with increased levels of co-creation and co-production. As a result, those products that allow us to define and verify our self-identities also experience increased probabilities and levels of growth.

Finally, as the adoption of many products grows, users see an increase in the utility of that product and the ability of that product to validate and define their identities. As we discussed with cell phones, the increase in adoption of cell phones meant that even more people who had not yet adopted them found them to be useful to connect with work, family, and friends. Similarly as social networks gain wider adoption the ability to connect with similar groups of people increases the usefulness of the tool as a communication mechanism and as a mechanism to define and verify identity. Therefore growth has a feedback loop both to *usefulness* and to *identity* within the viral model. As growth increases, the level of misuse also increases within the customer base, indicating that there is a feedback loop between growth and misuse within the model. Finally as misuse increases the ability of customers to define and verify their identity through misuse of the product increases, which indicates a feedback loop between misuse and identity. The viral model with associated feedback loops is shown again in Figure 5.2 below.

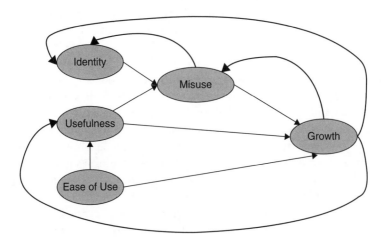

Figure 5.2 *Drivers of Viral Growth with Feedback*

PUTTING IT INTO PRACTICE

First and foremost, any company that aspires to achieving viral growth needs a key performance indicator (KPI) that monitors their progress towards achieving that objective. These companies should adopt the viral growth coefficient described in Chapter 1. Whether aspiring to viral growth, or simply higher levels of organic (non-sales driven or customer-to-customer referred) growth, we have presented several concepts that can be useful in your product development endeavors. Table 9.1 summarizes the factors, how to identify them and, most importantly, how to increase them in order to achieve viral growth.

Of critical importance to any product initiative is identifying how to increase innovation. Far too often we think of this as an activity that is necessarily internal to our firm; we seek to find ways to make our employees more innovative or to contribute in increasing levels to the innovation within our products. What we fail to do most often is look for innovation by our customers on our behalf. To be successful in this endeavor, we must be both vigilant and focused on identifying previously unforeseen usage within our products AND build processes around the enablement of such activity. Some of this is product-oriented work, building products that produce information around customer usage, and aggressively mining the resulting data for patterns that are inconsistent with the expected customer behavior. Ensuring that product engineers have design principles that call for the logging and storing of customer usage patterns early within a product lifecycle will help in this area.

Some of the work however is process related. It's not enough to log usage data. We must have a process around periodically (even daily) mining the data for emerging patterns. These patterns must be reviewed and analyzed thoroughly. The organization must equally importantly guard against the innate tendency to discount the value of the emerging pattern of usage to the firm, or hubristically argue against the enablement of the pattern as being inconsistent with the firm's grand vision for the product. To this end, executives must lead by example and remind the remainder of the company leadership of the value of such emerging customer behavior. Consider company principles or values that indicate *lead user* innovation within your product as the cheapest and highest quality innovation you can ever aspire to have.

Consider how you can allow users to help define and verify their self-identities within your firm's products. Consider the concepts of exhibitionism and voyeurism, both of which drive deeper user engagement and repeat visits (retention) and recommendations to other friends (fan-out). Allow individuals to discuss how your product or service is meaningful to their lives. Develop a sense of community, where

Table 9.1 *How to Make Use of the Model*

Factor	How to Identify	How to Increase
Viral growth	Viral coefficient (C_v) > 1	Leverage factors identified in the model (misuse, self-identity, ease of use, and usefulness).
Misuse	The company is actively watching for customer misbehavior and encouraging it.	Suppress hubris that you know how the product should be used.
		Watch how real customers use your product.
Co-creation	Users creating value of the product/service by using it (e.g. uploading pictures, making comments, etc.).	Build products that produce information around customer usage.
		Aggressively mine data for patterns that are inconsistent with the expected customer behavior.
Co-production	Users actively participating in the product/service design or creation process (e.g. selling a real Ferrari on eBay, putting Mentos candy in Diet Coke).	Ensure that product engineers have design principles that call for the logging and storing of customer usage patterns.
Self-identity	Individuals use the product to self-verify, express themselves, or join others with similar interests.	Allow users to customize the view that others will see of them.
		Disallow others to 'dislike' or 'disagree' with statements made by users.
		Develop a sense of community, where customers can bond over your product such that they can use it to describe themselves.
Ease of use	The product can be easily used by the intended audience as compared to other products / services in similar categories.	There are many resources available to help design ease of use into products and services such as:
		ISO/TR 16982:2002[13]
		ISO 9241[14]
		Lund's Usability Maxims[15]
		Human Factors and Ergonomics Society[16]
		Special Interest Group on Computer–Human Interaction[17]

(*continued*)

Table 9.1 *Continued*

Factor	How to Identify	How to Increase
Usefulness	The product successfully fills a need for users (e.g. facilitating social connections, entertainment, selling / buying products, researching).	There are many resources available for creating processes within an organization to ensure useful products are being built such as: A/B Testing[18] Iterative Design[19] Minimum Viable Product[20]

customers can have conversations related to your product such that they can use it to describe themselves. Within commerce sites, this may be commenting on products that you sell to describe where they use (or wear) your products and how they felt about using or wearing the product. In media sites, it may be discussing their feelings or beliefs about the media presented.

Recall that users also seek verification of their identities and tend to discard products and individuals that suggest inconsistent views (by others) of their identities. As such, you want to avoid allowing others to 'vote' that they 'dislike', 'hate', or 'disagree' with statements made by other users. It's OK to allow them to engage in discussions on topics and even disagreements, but you do not want to present easy to use functions that allow users to 'invalidate' each other's identities. Rather, implement features that allow easy validation of each other's identities to help engender greater usage.

Clearly we need to build products that are useful and easy to use. These concepts are well covered in other books and articles. That said, it is important to note that no product is likely to be adopted that is neither easy to use nor useful to an end user.

Build easy to use and useful products. Allow users to engage within your products by displaying and verifying their identities with others. Build products that allow users to contribute (often by displaying their identity) and co-produce your product (often through misuse) alongside you. Look for emerging trends of new, innovative, and previously unforeseen uses of your product and actively enable that usage. Then grow! Grow virally!

Appendix A: Viral Growth

CONTAGION

As we covered in Chapter 1, the concept of viral growth is derived from an epidemiological term relating to the spread of infectious disease. The primary concern that doctors and health care workers have with regards to contagious diseases is how the disease is transmitted in the population, and more specifically the transmission rate at which the disease will propagate through that population. This rate is highly dependent on factors such as the transmission mechanism, i.e. oral, sexual, vertical (mother-to-child). In order for the transmission of a disease to occur, two individuals must make contact via the transmission mechanism. Across an entire population, a total contact rate is the number of contacts per unit time, denoted γ in Equation 1. However not all contacts are effective, e.g. not everyone who comes into contact with an infected person becomes infected. Therefore the total contact rate needs to be multiplied by the probability of infection (also called the transmission risk) and is denoted p in Equation 1. The result, denoted as τ, is called the effective contact rate or the transmissibility of the disease.

$$\tau = y * p \qquad (1)$$

Using this transmissibility information we can calculate the basic reproduction number, R_0 – pronounced 'R-naught', which is the number of cases one case generates on average over the course of its infectious period. It is important to note that R_0 is a dimensionless number and not a rate, which would involve units of time. The other factors involved in the calculation are the average rate of contact between susceptible and infected individuals, denoted as c, and the duration of infectiousness represented as d in Equation 2 below.[1]

$$R_0 = \tau * c * d \qquad (2)$$

When $R_0 < 1$, the disease will die out in the long run. But if $R_0 > 1$, the disease is able to spread in a population. Measles, which is a highly contagious respiratory infection transmitted via airborne particles (think sneezes and coughs), has an R_0 of between 12 and 18. People sharing a living space with a person infected with the measles will catch it 90 per cent of the time (p from Equation 1).[2] The flu which we battle each year is caused by the influenza virus and has an R_0 greater than 1, allowing it to spread throughout the population. One of the worst influenza infections was the 1918 pandemic, which infected 500 million people and killed between 20 to 50 million. It is estimated that it had an R_0 between 1.3 and 3.1.[3]

POSSIBLE ACTIONS

The viral growth equations discussed in Chapter 1 suggest several alternative ways in which a product or service provider can succeed or fail to achieve viral growth. New product characteristics such as service breadth (how many features the product has) and service quality (how good the products are) clearly increase retention rate.[4] Similarly, if the adoption rate is not sufficiently high (driven by fan-out and conversion), or if existing users are leaving faster than they can be replaced (driven by retention rate), sustained viral growth will not result. Moreover the nature of services and the length of the frequency of the cycle affect the service growth. If we can entice users to use or consume the product or service multiple times per day we are able to achieve more opportunities that others will see them using the service and ask about it, or for the users themselves to realize they should recommend it to others.

PARETO DISTRIBUTION

One final point that will help us to understand the term *viral growth*. If you are familiar with the Pareto principle you will notice that the viral growth distribution looks very similar to a Pareto distribution. That is because Pareto distributions also follow power laws. Vilfredo Federico Damaso Pareto was an Italian economist who lived from 1848 to 1923, and was responsible for contributing several important advances to economics. Fascinated by power and wealth distribution in societies, he studied the property ownership in Italy and observed in his 1909 publication that 20 per cent of the population owned 80 per cent of the land, thus giving rise to the famous Pareto Distribution. Technically, the Pareto Distribution expresses a power law of a probability distribution, which follows a special relationship between the frequency of an observed event (20 per cent of population are land owners) and the size of the event (80 per cent of the land owned by these people). [5] Another power law is Kleiber's Law of metabolism that states that the metabolic rate of an animal scales to the 3/4 power of the mass. As an example a horse that is 50 times larger than a rabbit will have a metabolism 18.8 times greater than the rabbit.

Appendix B: A Short Summary of Research Informing the Book Findings

This appendix offers a detailed explanation of the research study that developed the original model of the effects of self-identity and the impact of co-creation and co-production on the growth of social networking sites. This is the study we refer to as the author's PhD study in the main body of text. We also report below how we tested and validated major parts of the model that is formulated and discussed in the book. In this appendix we cover three sections – research methodology and approach, overview of main results, and key papers stemming from the research, for readers who want to find out more about the details of the findings and research methods.

RESEARCH METHODOLOGY

Research Design

We used in the study a mixed methods approach which has been called the third path.[1] It has recently emerged as an alternative to overcome the fruitless dichotomy of qualitative and quantitative approaches.[2] Johnson, Onwuegbuzie, and Turner[3] define mixed methods research as:

> Mixed methods research is the type of research in which a researcher or team of researchers combines elements of qualitative and quantitative research approaches (e.g. use of qualitative and quantitative viewpoints, data collection, analysis, inference techniques) for the broad purposes of breadth and depth of understanding and corroboration.

There are at least five purposes for mixed method approaches – triangulation, completeness, development, initiation, and expansion.[4]

In our study context, development and triangulation were two main motivations for using a mixed method design, given the fact that we explored unchartered terrain – what consumer behaviors contribute to viral growth. Development – broadly construed to include sampling and measurement decisions – seeks to use the results from one method to develop or inform the other method.[5] In our study this motivated us to utilize qualitative methods and analysis to inform our quantitative track. Triangulation refers to 'the designed use of multiple methods, with offsetting or counteracting biases, in investigations of the same phenomenon in order to strengthen the validity of inquiry results'.[6] In our study context, the motivation was to ensure we generate the strongest validation of the emergent theory by utilizing two approaches with differing strengths as to acquire analysis and validation results.[7] The core premise of triangulation is that all methods have inherent biases and limitations; therefore, two or more methods that have offsetting biases provide findings that have enhanced validity.

Mixed method research does not necessarily align with a single inferential system or philosophy,[8] because of its pragmatic roots.[9] It's use is primarily driven by a pragmatic, problem driven research question – like ours – rather than being first restrained by paradigmatic and stringent theoretical assumptions.[10] We assessed from the start that our research problem was ideally suited for a mixed methodology study as we were interested in understanding an emerging and new phenomenon in a context. Additionally our study involved interactions between individuals' attitudes and behaviors within a socially complex environment, consisting of social networking platforms that facilitate these interactions. In this sense our study was a multi-level study that is better suited to be examined using a mixed method approach. Finally, the analysis of some of the direct effects of individual and social behaviors on the dependent variables of fan-out and retention on a Social Networking Site (SNS) were ideally suited for a quantitative analysis.

Our research program was divided into three separate studies as diagramed in Figure A.1. The study began by seeking to explain the differences in viral growth between two SNS platforms. In particular we asked: what are the underlying user behaviors that could explain those differences? Because of the lack of a theory to adequately explain these differences from both the user and platform provider perspectives, we engaged first in exploratory theory development using a qualitative grounded theory approach.[11] This resulted in a model of social exchanges and identity as one of the key drivers of SNS growth.

Informed by insights from this study, we next compared and contrasted the differences between the social exchange model and the classic Technology Acceptance Model (TAM) in explaining the viral growth. Here we utilized a quantitative approach. We thereby were able to formulate a more focused set of research questions to explore underlying mechanisms that explain the level and nature of user interactions on a SNS and how these explain platform growth. Our third study dived deeper into the variations in user behaviors within and between social networking sites. Again this analysis was informed by the results of the qualitative study. Combined, these three studies helped formulate and validate a theory of viral growth of digital platforms through one theory generation and validation cycle, and offer empirical validation and results that informed writing several critical sections of the book.

We will next adopt a sequential (Qual→Quant sequence model according to Morse's Notation[12]) development and triangulation mixed methods model, where an exploratory qualitative study is conducted prior to a quantitative study, but where through several revisions and cross-referencing of data and results the studies are combined to strengthen and inform each other (Figure A.2). The qualitative strand involved conducting semi-structured phenomenological interviews with users and executives of SNS platforms. The product from this – codes, themes, and theory – informed subsequent quantitative model development. Additionally the results of the quantitative study were cross-

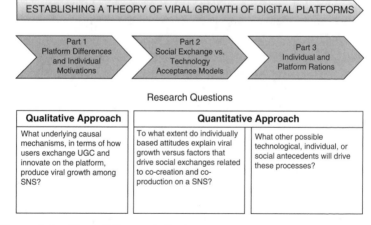

Figure A.1   *Overall Research Design*

Note: UGC – User-Generated Content; SNS – Social Networking Site.

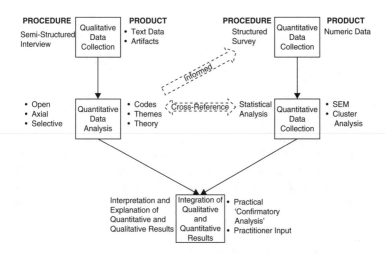

Figure A.2 *Triangulation Mixed Method Research Model*

referenced with the qualitative results to further explain the results in the final integration. This triangulation of results and theory utilized the qualitative observations to guide the quantitative study and then help clarify the quantitative results, allowing for much deeper and contextually valid insights.[13] In this manner, we benefited from mixing methods sequentially where each method – qualitative and quantitative – has equal standing. Both strands are explained next in more detail.

Qualitative Strand

As described by Strauss and Corbin,[14] the qualitative method 'allows researchers to get at the inner experience of participants, to determine how meanings are formed through and in culture'. We sought to discern and examine possible relationships between product attributes and individuals' attitudes or behaviors that increased viral growth – fan-out, conversion, and retention rates – of SNS. Phenomenological, semi-structured interviews, informed by grounded theory principles,[15] were conducted with customers of Facebook and Friendster. Semi-structured interviews allowed for structure and uniformity in the collection of data, but preserved flexibility and opportunity for the emergence of novel contributions from respondents. We interviewed both users as well as executives of two SNS in order to obtain a robust set of data to analyze.

Our sample consisted of 29 SNS users – 19 Facebook subscribers and 10 members of Friendster. A second group of respondents included two former executives of Friendster, two current/former executives of Facebook, and one consultant who worked with both Facebook and Friendster.

The data was analyzed using grounded theory methods recommended by Strauss and Corbin,[16] including constant comparison and theoretical sampling. Emergent themes and concepts directed forward sampling, which continued until no more themes, or concepts, could be identified, signaling theoretical saturation. From this analysis we developed a conceptual model of viral growth that became the basis of the first hypothesized model that was then validated via the quantitative methods.

Qualitative Data Analysis

Data analysis began after the first interview. All recorded interviews were listened to, transcribed, and the transcripts read several times. Thereafter we followed the recommendations of Strauss and Corbin (1990) and conducted three iterative phases of coding: open, axial, and selective. During the first phase of open coding we examined each transcript line by line to identify fragments of text. These fragments were labeled and cross-referenced with excerpts from prior transcripts.

Open coding resulted in the identification of 534 codes later grouped into 24 categories relating to user retention, product attributes, new users joining, or strong emotion. During the second phase of analysis, axial coding, we refined these emergent themes by defining their properties and dimensions, a process that later reduced them to the 19 themes shown in Table A.1 below. During the final phase of analysis, selective coding, we focused on nine key themes, identified in Table A.1 as 'selected', that yielded the five findings reported in the next section.

Quantitative Strand

To empirically test the proposed model, we surveyed users of five of the 2010 top social networking sites – Facebook, Twitter, LinkedIn, Myspace, and Ning[17] – and three social networks that had failed to achieve sustained viral growth in the United States (e.g. Friendster, Yahoo! 360, and Orkut). We followed a psychometric survey

Table A.1   *Original and Selected Themes*

Number	Theme	Selected
1	Association prestige of connecting with a special person	*
2	Concerned about the lack of ability to use technology	
3	Concerned about the security of private information	
4	Conforming to etiquettes	*
5	Continuum of intimacy using different technologies	
6	Creepiness detracts from enjoyment	
7	Ease of use	
8	Emotional reaction to technology	
9	Live vicariously by using virtual reality	*
10	Minimize isolation and feel connected	*
11	Need to feel in control of the technology	*
12	Peer pressure to join	
13	Performance of site	
14	Reputation management	*
15	Self-perception influences adoption and usage	
16	Sharing fun and entertainment with friends	*
17	Usefulness	
18	Using technology to sustain relationships	*
19	Voyeurism and exhibitionism	*

methodology that maps individual responses to the underlying constructs within our model. Our model involved 11 constructs all of which were measured with reflective scales.

We used a 'snowballing' technique to reach a diverse sample of SNS users. Two primary approaches were used to collect data. First, we leveraged the personal and professional network of the researchers by posting the link to the survey on the social networks being studied asking for participation and for assistance distributing the request by reposting to their networks. This 'snowballing' technique is amenable to the same scientific sampling procedures as ordinary sample.[18] Using this method we received 432 responses. Second, we distributed the survey via email to 229 undergraduate and 618 graduate students at a mid-western research university. We received 343 completed responses. To maximize response rates, we guaranteed anonymity, collected no personally identifiable information, and assured respondents that only the researchers would have access to the raw data. In total, we received 775 respondents, with a 14.1 per cent dropout rate, categorized as such if more than 10 per cent of the responses were missing. The remaining

666 respondents provided 1449 cases for analysis as respondents answered for multiple social networks.

Structural equation modeling (SEM) provides the ability to simultaneously estimate multiple dependent relationships and incorporate multiple items for each of the concepts.[19] This study followed a two-step SEM approach as recommended by Anderson and Gerbing,[20] where a factor analysis based measurement model specifies first the relationships of the observed measures to their posited underlying constructs and then a confirmatory structural model which specifies and estimates the causal relations of the constructs with one another.

Quantitative Measurement Model

The data was initially screened for missing data, outliers, normality, linearity, homoscedasticity, and multicollinearity. No significant threats were found. Then it was split randomly into two sets (750 data points in set 1, and 699 data points in set 2). The first set was used to conduct an Exploratory Factor Analysis (EFA) while the second set for conducting Confirmatory Factor Analysis (CFA) and testing the Structural Model.

Using EFA, an 11 factor unconstrained solution emerged with eigenvalues greater than 1.0 that collectively explained 65 per cent of the total variance. This informed our CFA model, resulting in the solution reported in Table A.2. The fit statistics were acceptable; factor loadings for all items were statistically significant and ranged from 0.504 to 0.985; composite reliability for each construct exceeded 0.70, except for two on the margin at 0.68 and 0.69; the average variance extracted (AVE) was above 0.50 (convergent validity); and the square-roots of all AVEs were greater than the correlations between the respective construct and other constructs (discriminant validity).[21]

As a singular method was used to tap into all constructs, we used post hoc statistical tests to detect the threat of Common Method Bias (CMB). First, we used Harman's single-factor test[22] using Principal Component Analysis, which resulted in an 11 factor solution where the first extracted factor explained 29.5 per cent of the variance.[23] Second, we created a CFA model with a common factor[24] using a random sample of 300 data points, as to offer a base for 'more strict evaluation'.[25] The common factor extracted only 5.4 per cent of the variance suggesting a lack of CMB. In addition, a χ^2 difference test (χ^2= 2.371; df=1, p = 0.124) between the baseline model with all the CMB paths

Constructs	1.	2.	3.	4.	5.	6.	7.	8.	9.	10.	11.	Range of Factor Loadings	CR	AVE	MSV	ASV
1. Perceived Usefulness	0.82											0.75–0.81	0.81	0.67	0.46	0.21
2. Fan-out	0.63	0.85										0.68–0.94	0.83	0.72	0.72	0.26
3. Retention	0.71	0.81	0.85									0.65–0.99	0.93	0.72	0.72	0.25
4. Co-creation	0.51	0.53	0.45	0.84								0.74–0.86	0.83	0.71	0.44	0.22
5. Co-production	0.27	0.49	0.23	0.70	0.72							0.66–0.71	0.68	0.52	0.44	0.21
6. Perceived Ease of Use	0.58	0.36	0.53	0.38	0.07	0.82						0.65–0.87	0.89	0.68	0.39	0.17
7. User Interface	0.51	0.48	0.58	0.39	0.29	0.68	0.82					0.71–0.81	0.81	0.68	0.39	0.21
8. Privacy Policy	0.10	0.08	0.13	0.15	0.23	0.14	0.39	0.79				0.58–0.85	0.83	0.63	0.16	0.07
9. Page Load Time	0.16	0.16	0.40	0.03	-0.28	0.26	0.35	-0.02	0.73			0.45–0.79	0.69	0.54	0.24	0.12
10. Exhibitionism	-0.02	0.06	-0.16	0.21	0.54	-0.22	-0.16	-0.16	-0.45	0.72		0.38–0.71	0.81	0.52	0.43	0.13
11. Voyeurism	0.03	-0.01	-.16	0.04	0.32	-0.13	-0.10	-0.17	-0.33	0.68	0.88	0.77–0.90	0.87	0.77	0.39	0.07

Notes: Model fit indices: X^2 (df) = 830.716 (347), p = 0.000; root mean square error of approximation (RMSEA) = 0.043, standardized root mean square residual (SRMR) = 0.036, normed fit index (NFI) = 0.917, goodness-of-fit index (GFI) = 0.904, adjusted goodness-of-fit index (AGFI) = 0.876, comparative fit index (CFI) = 0.967. Square-root of AVE values along the diagonal.

free floating, and the CMB model with all paths equal to zero, was not significant.

Three structural equation models using maximum likelihood estimation were specified in AMOS[26] – individual, social exchange model, and combined model – to test the significance of the hypothesized paths. The final fit statistics for each structural model ranged from very good to outstanding[27] – see Table A.3. When testing the consecutive models we compared changes in the significance of path coefficients and R squares as to evaluate model parsimony, changes in causal logic and explanatory power. The final results of the tests are reported below for the combined model. This is followed with a discussion of observed significant model differences. Mediation tests followed Baron-Kenny method.[28] We used bootstrapping with 1000 samples to test for the statistical significance of the postulated indirect effects using 95 per cent confidence interval.[29] For multi-path mediation we applied Shrout and Bolger[30] and Fletcher's[31] tests.[32]

OVERVIEW OF MAIN RESULTS

As discussed above our research was divided into three studies as diagramed in Figure A.2. The main results of these three studies are discussed below.

Study 1: The Co-Production of Viral Growth: A Comparative Analysis of Two SNS

We discerned and examined possible relationships between individual, social, and technological factors such as individuals' attitudes and behaviors that increased the viral growth of SNS through fan-out, conversion, and retention. We also sought out organizational processes that enable the SNS platform to modify and adapt its components to service the need of the individuals. We identified that Facebook and Friendster had significantly different approaches to product development, which led to very dissimilar user experiences. The expression of user's self-identity was supported on Facebook, as demonstrated by the executive who stated, 'we see one of our core use cases [as being] identity and identity management.' Facebook users confirmed that they constructed their self-identity through behaviors including the development and

Table A.3 *Model Fit Statistics for Structural Analysis*

Model Fit Statistics	Modified TAM	Social Exchange Model	Combined Model	Typical Threshold
Chi Square (DF)	0.072 (1)	0.672 (1)	62.034 (30)	
Probability	0.788	.412	.001	<0.05
Sample Size (n)	699	699	699	> 5*(items)
CMIN/DF	0.072	0.672	2.068	< 2.0
CFI	1.000	1.000	0.994	> 0.95
PCFI	0.167	0.036	0.328	> 0.5
RMSEA (LO 90 – HI 90)	0.000 (.000–.065)	0.000 (.000–.090)	0.039 (.025–.053)	< 0.05
PCLOSE	0.910	0.723	0.899	> 0.5
SRMR	0.0012	0.0038	0.0218	< 0.09

maintenance of relationships, sharing, controlling diverse worlds, reputation management, and living vicariously.

Study 2: The Antecedents of Viral Growth on Social Networking Platforms

In this study we attempted to answer our second research question: to what extent do individually-based attitudes explain viral growth, versus factors that drive social exchanges related to co-creation and co-production on a SNS? We first wanted to know how much explanatory power TAM has on explaining viral growth due to the fact that SNS platforms are considered a type of innovative technology for single users to adopt and use. The antecedents of adoption in TAM – perceived usefulness and ease of use – were posited to predict the user behaviors of fan-out and retention, not just their intention to adopt. We next desired to determine to what extent individually based psychological motivators – voyeurism and exhibitionism – expanded from the self-identity factors explained viral growth. Additionally, we wanted to investigate how participation in co-creation and co-production mediates or directly influences viral growth. To this end, we developed a set of hypotheses and constructed three hypothesized model including a mediated model.

The first model was a modified TAM model where antecedents of page load time, user interface, and privacy policy influenced perceived usefulness and perceived ease of use which influence fan-out and retention. The second model was the Social Exchange model that hypothesized that the processes of co-creation and co-production will mediate the effect of voyeurism and exhibitionism on fan-out and retention. The third model was the 'blended' or combined model that integrated the TAM and Social Exchange models.

The TAM model resulted in very good explanatory power of 42 per cent and 56 per cent and the overall predictive power was similar to the results associated with TAM3 (Venkatesh and Bala[33]). Our combined model demonstrated greater explanatory power – 56 per cent and 65 per cent explained variance for fan-out and retention – demonstrating a 16 per cent and 33 per cent improvement over the modified TAM model alone. Calculating the squared partial correlations as recommended by Cohen[34] we measured $f^2 = 0.24$ for fan-out and $f^2 = 0.20$ for retention, both representing between medium and large differences in the R^2 of the models. The final structural model is shown in Figure A.3 below.

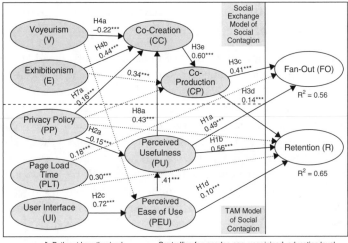

Figure A.3   *Structural Model*

<u>Perceived ease of use.</u> Our results indicated that perceived ease of use was not a significant predictor of fan-out behavior.

<u>Page load time.</u> We found that page load time was a significant direct predictor of fan-out ($\beta = 0.16$, p< 0.001) and retention ($\beta = 0.26$, $p < 0.001$).

<u>Co-production.</u> The level of co-production did not affect retention, but did affect fan-out. We did find support for a chained mediation from exhibitionism through co-creation and co-production to retention. Our finding suggests that co-creation is a significant antecedent to co-production (in contrast to service dominant logic models).[35]

<u>Self-identity.</u> Voyeurism had a *negative effect* on fan-out and retention indirectly through co-creation. In contrast, exhibitionism was found to have a *positive direct effect* on both retention and fan-out; and it partially mediated positively through co-creation and co-production, in the combined model. Our findings support earlier research and build upon it by demonstrating the distal mediation of exhibitionism on retention and fan-out is chained through both co-creation and co-production.[36] Users who are mostly exhibitionists drive fan-out and are critical for viral growth, as they want others to see what they do.

Study 3: The Influence of User Mix on the Viral Growth of Social Networking Sites

In this study we desired to further understand our second research question: what other possible technological, individual, or social antecedents will drive the co-creation and co-production processes? Guided by the conceptual model developed from the qualitative study we hypothesized and tested a more refined research model that extended the findings from the first quantitative study. We utilized the results of our qualitative study to assist in explaining our findings. Our objective was specifically to explore how the individual and the network level observed ratios of voyeurism to exhibitionism in user-level motivations affect viral growth. In particular, we investigated the moderating and interaction effects of the individual SNS platform as well as the voyeurism/exhibitionism ratio. We used the same data set as in the first study. We used the clustering method to identify groups of users *within* and *between* users on a SNS with different voyeurism and exhibitionism profiles. We utilized structural equation modeling (SEM) for data analysis to study the causality between model elements.

Our results revealed that the level of voyeuristic and exhibitionistic behavior varies depending on which SNS the users are participating in and thus the level of voyeuristic and exhibitionistic behaviors is extrinsic and depends on the network and its functionality. Thus SNS should strive to facilitate users to manifest the ratio of voyeurism and exhibitionism that most promotes fan-out and retention. The next logical question is what amount of voyeurism and exhibitionism is most likely to produce sustained viral growth? Not surprising, we found that unengaged users had little effect on fan-out and retention, whereas users with a ratio of high voyeurism and medium exhibitionism had stronger effect on retention. We identified also that regardless of the level of exhibitionism, the level of voyeurism predicted the fan-out – *low* voyeurism equated to *low* fan-out while *high* voyeurism equated to *high* fan-out. Thus the SNS attempting to achieve sustained viral growth should attempt to produce a platform that facilitates high levels of voyeurism and a moderate (medium) amount of exhibitionism. This combination appears to be the most likely to produce high levels of fan-out and sustained retention.

Summary of Findings

In summary, we found through three studies that factors that facilitate co-creation of user generated content on social networking sites, and behaviors involved in the creation and management of one's self-identity were significant drivers of viral growth (of SNS). We have further identified that the combination of these individual behaviors and platform processes are better predictors of viral growth than the TAM alone. Specifically, we found also that voyeurism, a behavior associated with self-identity, has a *negative effect* on fan-out and retention when mediated through co-creation whereas exhibitionism, also associated with self-identity, has a *positive direct effect* on both retention and fan-out, partially mediated through co-creation and co-production. Our findings further suggest that the level of voyeuristic and exhibitionistic behavior varies depending on which SNS the users are participating in and thus is extrinsic. Further, it was demonstrated that when users are 'matched' with the SNS in terms of having similar voyeuristic-to-exhibitionistic ratios there was greater fan-out and retention. We found that, as expected, unengaged users have little effect on fan-out and retention, whereas users with a ratio of high voyeurism and medium exhibitionism have a strong effect on retention. And lastly, we identified that regardless of the level of exhibitionism, the level of voyeurism predicted the fan-out – low voyeurism equated to low fan-out while high voyeurism equated to high fan-out.

RESEARCH PAPERS

The following conference papers and journal articles detail the key findings:

M. Fisher et al. (2011) 'The Co-production of Social Contagion: A Comparative Analysis of Two Social Networking Sites', Academy of Management OCIS E-commerce and Service Innovation Session.

M. Fisher et al. (2011) 'The Underlying Causal Mechanisms Affecting Social Contagion of Digital Content Service Platforms', Engaged Management Scholarship Conference, Doctoral Consortium.

M. Fisher, K. Lyytinen, R. Boland (2012) 'It's All about Identity: Explaining Viral Growth on Social Networking Sites', Unpublished working paper, Case Western Reserve University.

M. Fisher, K. Lyytinen, T. Somers (2013) 'Exploring Social Networking Site Use: The Effects of Voyeurism, Exhibitionism, and Co-Creation on Viral Growth', Unpublished working paper, Case Western Reserve University.

M. Fisher, M. Abbott, K. Lyytinen (2013) 'Moving from Misuse to Bricolage: Finding Innovation from Customer "Misbehavior" ', *Graziadio Business Review*, **16**(1).

Glossary

Bricolage – a French term indicating unexpected usage of a product. The authors present this as a more appropriate way to think of customer misbehavior, or misuse of products.

Co-creation – the process of users constructing their own experiences through personalized interaction, such as user-generated content on a social networking site or content creation in the form of comments left on a blog.

Conversion rate – number of new users converted to using the service.

Co-production – the activity of contributing or modifying the product or service offering itself.

Fan-out – number of new users invited per existing user.

Misbehavior (Misuse) – the result of customer's misbehaving when performing uninvited co-production.

Perceived ease of use – the degree to which a person believes that using a specific technology will be free from effort.

Perceived usefulness – the degree to which a person believes that using a specific technology will improve his or her performance of a particular task.

Self-identity – A collection of beliefs about oneself that creates the awareness of oneself as a separate individual.

Technology Acceptance Model (TAM) – a theory that models how users accept a new technology with the constructs of Perceived ease of use and Perceived usefulness as primary drivers of the behavioral intent.

Vicious cycle – a chain of events that reinforces itself with detrimental results for a person or company – the opposite of a Virtuous cycle.

Viral coefficient (C_v) – similar to basic reproductive rate (R_0) in that it predicts the number of new users that will be generated by one existing user through influencing, recommending, suggesting, sharing, and so on. This results from the multiplication of the variables, Fan-out and Conversion rate.

Viral growth – the increase in the user base of a product or service, resulting from people's action to induce other people in their networks to repeat their usage of the product or service.

Virtuous cycle – a chain of events, resulting in a favorable outcome that reinforces itself through a feedback loop.

Notes and References

INTRODUCTION

1. United States Census Bureau (2012) *Wholesale & Retail Trade: Motor Vehicle Sales*, p. 663.
2. 'By Owner' Used Car Sales Soar. 2004, available from: http://www.theautochannel.com/news/2004/05/05/193445.html.
3. N. Franke and E. Von Hippel (2003) 'Satisfying heterogeneous user needs via innovation toolkits: the case of Apache security software', *Research Policy*, **32**(7), pp. 1199–215; E. Von Hippel, S. Thomke and M. Sonnack (1999) 'Creating breakthroughs at 3M', *Harvard Business Review*, 77, pp. 47–57.
4. Von Hippel et al., 'Creating breakthroughs at 3M'.
5. M.E. Adams, G. S. Day and D. Dougherty (1998) 'Enhancing New Product Development Performance: An Organizational Learning Perspective', *Journal of Product Innovation Management*, **15**(5), pp. 403–22.
6. S. Diller, N. Shedroff and D. Rhea (2006) *Making Meaning: How Successful Businesses Deliver Meaningful Customer Experiences* (New Riders).
7. C. Mackay (1841) *Extraordinary Popular Delusions and the Madness of Crowds* (Barnes & Noble Library of Essential Reading); G. Le Bon (1897) *The Crowd: A Study of the Popular Mind* (Macmillian).
8. A. L. Penenberg (2009) *Viral Loop: From Facebook to Twitter, How Today's Smartest Businesses Grow Themselves*, First ed. (New York: Hyperion).
9. G. Fowler, 'Facebook: One Billion and Counting', *Wall Street Journal*, 4 Oct. 2012.
10. M. Chafkin, 'How to Kill a Great Idea!', 1 June 2007, available from: http://www.inc.com/magazine/20070601/features-how-to-kill-a-great-idea.html.
11. S. Olsen, 'Google's Antisocial Downside', 13 July 2006, available from: http://news.cnet.com/Googles-antisocial-downside/2100-1038_3-6093532.html; P. Cashmore (2006) 'Myspace, America's Number

One', available from http://mashable.com/2006/07/11/myspace-americas-number-one/.

12. A. Fixmer, 'News Corp. Calls Quits on Myspace with Specific Media Sale', *Business Week*, 29 June 2011, available from: http://www.businessweek.com/news/2011-06-29/news-corp-calls-quits-on-myspace-with-specific-media-sale.html.

13. A. Kambil, G. Friesen and A. Sundaram (1999) 'Co-creation: A new source of value', *Outlook Magazine*, 3(2), pp. 23–9; V. Zwass (2010) 'Co-creation: toward a taxonomy and an integrated research perspective', *International Journal of Electronic Commerce*, 15(1), pp. 11–48; S. Vargo, P. Maglio and M. Akaka (2008) 'On value and value co-creation: A service systems and service logic perspective', *European Management Journal*, 26(3), pp. 145–52.

14. S. Wikström (1996) 'The customer as co-producer', *European Journal of Marketing*, 30(4), pp. 6–19.

15. F. D. Davis (1989) 'Perceived usefulness, perceived ease of use, and user acceptance of information technology', *MIS Quarterly*, pp. 319–40.

16. ibid.

17. S. Stryker (1980) *Symbolic Interactionism: A Social Structural Version* (Benjamin/Cummings Publishing Company); S. Stryker (1987) 'Identity theory: Developments and extensions', in K. Yardley, T. Honess (eds) *Self and Identity: Psychosocial Perspectives* (Oxford, England) pp. 89–103; S. Stryker and P. J. Burke (2000) 'The past, present, and future of an identity theory', *Social Psychology Quarterly*, pp. 284–97; Y. Lee, J. Lee and Z. Lee (2006) 'Social influence on technology acceptance behavior: self-identity theory perspective', ACM SIGMIS Database 37.2–3, pp. 60–75; P. Sparks and C. A. Guthrie (1998) 'Self-Identity and the Theory of Planned Behavior: A Useful Addition or an Unhelpful Artifice?', *Journal of Applied Social Psychology*, 28(15), pp. 1393–410.

18. Davis, 'Perceived usefulness'.

1 WHY IS VIRAL GROWTH IMPORTANT?

1. See YouTube, http://www.youtube.com/watch?v=4r7wHMg5Yjg

2. 'Honey Badger Don't Care...About New TV Show', *New York Observer*, http://observer.com/2012/01/honey-badger-dont-care-about-new-tv-show/

3. See Twitter, https://twitter.com/czgordon

4. 'A Chat With Randall: On Nasty Honey Badgers, Bernie Madoff And Fame', *Forbes Magazine*, 21 Apr. 2011, http://www.forbes.com/sites/michaelhumphrey/2011/04/21/a-chat-with-randall-on-nasty-honey-badgers-bernie-madoff-and-fame/

5. See KnowYourMeme, http://knowyourmeme.com/memes/honey-badger#fn2

6. Interest over time. Web Search for 'honey badger', worldwide, 2004–13, http://www.google.com/trends/explore#q=%22honey%20badger%22&cmpt=q

7. S. Jurvetson (2000) 'What exactly is viral marketing', *Red Herring*, 78, pp. 110–12.

8. A. L. Penenberg (2009) *Viral Loop: From Facebook to Twitter, How Today's Smartest Businesses Grow Themselves*, First ed. (New York: Hyperion).

9. M. E. J. Newman (2005) 'Power laws, Pareto distributions and Zipf's law', *Contemporary Physics*, **46**(5), pp. 323–51.

10. According to the online Merriam-Webster dictionary, http://www.merriam-webster.com/dictionary/contagion

11. K. Kalyanam (2007) 'Adaptive experimentation in interactive marketing: The case of viral marketing at Plaxo', *Journal of Interactive Marketing*, **21**(3), p. 72.

12. Penenberg, *Viral Loop*.

13. M. Cha et al. (2008) *Characterizing social cascades in flickr* (ACM).

14. B. Tedeschi, 'Easier to use sites would help e-tailers close more sales', *The New York Times*, 12 June 2000.

15. H. H. Kuan, G. W. Bock and V. Vathanophas, (2005) 'Comparing the effects of usability on customer conversion and retention at e-commerce websites' (ACM).

16. J. Kim and S. Forsythe (2007) 'Hedonic usage of product virtualization technologies in online apparel shopping', *International Journal of Retail & Distribution Management*, **35**(6), pp. 502–14.

17. As reported by Nielsen Online, see http://blog.nielsen.com/nielsenwire/online_mobile/twitters-tweet-smell-of-success/

18. See Inc., 'How to Kill a Great Idea!' http://www.inc.com/magazine/20070601/features-how-to-kill-a-great-idea.html

19. 'Facebook's June 2010 US Traffic by Age and Sex: Users Aged 18–44 Take a Growth Break', available from: http://www.insidefacebook.com/2010/07/06/facebooks-june-2010-us-traffic-by-age-and-sex-users-aged-18-44-take-a-break-2/

20. L. Backstrom (2011) 'Anatomy of Facebook', [cited 15 July 2013], available from https://www.facebook.com/notes/facebook-data-team/anatomy-of-facebook/10150388519243859

21. Penenberg, *Viral Loop*.

22. C. Lewis and J. Neville (1995) 'Images of Rosie: A Content Analysis of Women Workers in American Magazine Advertising, 1940–1946', *Journalism & Mass Communication Quarterly*, 72(1), pp. 216–27.

23. L. Italie, 'Still Fresh: Tupperware enjoys renaissance after 65 years on market', *Eagle Tribune*, 2011.

24. Reproduced with permission of CSI © 2009. Data Source: CSI www.csidata.com/

25. Search engine optimization (SEO) is the process of improving a website's placement in a search engine's 'natural', or un-paid, search results.

26. R. Vohra (2012) 'How to Model Viral Growth: The Hybrid Model' [cited 30 Jan. 2013], available from: http://www.linkedin.com/today/post/article/20121002124206-18876785-how-to-model-viral-growth-the-hybrid-model.

27. S. Goel, D. J. Watts and D. G. Goldstein (2012) 'The structure of online diffusion networks', in *Proceedings of the 13th ACM Conference on Electronic Commerce* (ACM).

28. See Sharad Goel, 'The Structure of Online Diffusion Networks', https://www.youtube.com/watch?v=UdNYvjxpEvU

2   TECHNOLOGICAL FACTORS

1. E. Rogers (1962) *Diffusion of Innovations* (Free Press).

2. E. M. Rogers, A. Singhal and M. M. Quinlan (2009) 'Diffusion of Innovation', in M. B. Salwen (ed.) *An Integrated Approach to Communication Theory and Research* (Taylor & Francis), pp. 418–34.

3. B. Ryan and N. C. Gross (1943) 'The diffusion of hybrid seed corn in two Iowa communities', *Rural Sociology*, 8(1), pp. 15–24.

4. Rogers et al., 'Diffusion of Innovation'.

5. E. Rogers and D. Kincaid (1981) *Communication Networks: Toward a New Paradigm for Research* (New York: Free Press).

6. See Wikipedia, 'Carroll, Iowa', http://en.wikipedia.org/wiki/Carroll,_Iowa

7. A. Singhal (2005) 'Forum: The life and work of Everett Rogers – some personal reflections', [Electronic Version], *Journal of Health Communication*, **10**, pp. 285–8.

8. G. M. Beal, E. M. Rogers and J. M. Bohlen (1957) 'Validity of the Concept of Stages in the Adoption Process', *Rural Sociology*, **22**(2), pp. 166–8.

9. G. M. Beal and J. M. Bohlen (1957) *The Diffusion Process* (Iowa State College: Agricultural Experiment Station).

10. G. A. Moore (2002) *Crossing the Chasm: Marketing and Selling Disruptive Products to Mainstream Customers* (HarperBusiness).

11. J. Hale, B. Householder and K. Greene (2003) *The Theory of Reasoned Action: Developments in Theory and Practice* (Thousand Oaks, CA: Sage).

12. F. Davis (1989) 'Perceived usefulness, perceived ease of use, and user acceptance of information technology', *MIS Quarterly*, **13**(3), pp. 319–40.

13. F. Davis, R. Bagozzi and P. Warshaw (1989) User acceptance of computer technology: a comparison of two theoretical models', *Management Science*, **35**(8), pp. 982–1003.

14. Davis et al., 'User acceptance of computer technology'.

15. Davis, 'Perceived usefulness'.

16. R. L. Schultz and D. P. Slevin (1973) *Implementation and Organizational Validity: An Empirical Investigation* (Institute for Research in the Behavioral, Economic, and Management Sciences, Purdue University).

17. Davis, 'Perceived usefulness'.

18. M. Sigala et al. (2000) 'The diffusion and application of multimedia technologies in the tourism and hospitality industries', in *Information and Communication Technologies in Tourism 2000* (Springer) pp. 396–407.

19. M. Chuttur (2009) 'Overview of the technology acceptance model: Origins, developments and future directions', *Sprouts Working Papers on Information Systems*, **9**(37) (Indiana University).

20. V. Venkatesh and H. Bala (2008) 'Technology acceptance model 3 and a research agenda on interventions', *Decision Sciences*, **39**(2), p. 273.

21. R. P. Bagozzi, F. D. Davis and P. R.Warshaw (1992) 'Development and Test of a Theory of Technological Learning and Usage', *Human Relations*, **45**(7), pp. 659–86.

22. R. P. Bagozzi (2007) 'The Legacy of the Technology Acceptance Model and a Proposal for a Paradigm Shift', *Journal of the Association for Information Systems*, 8(4), p. 3.

3 THE VIRAL MODEL

1. 'Our Story' [Kubxlab Company Story], available from: http://www.kubxlab.com/pages/our-story

2. A. Deutschman (2001) *The Second Coming of Steve Jobs* (Broadway).

3. *iPod Nano 1.2 Firmware* (2011) YouTube. pp. 2–25.

4. Apple Special Event 2012, iPod Nano 7th Generation Introduction, www.youtube.com.

5. K. Butler (2013) 'Apple testing new smartwatch, rumored "iWatch"', www.upi.com

6. R. S. Burt (2005) *Brokerage and Closure: An Introduction to Social Capital* (Oxford University Press).

7. ibid.

8. C. K. Prahalad and V. Ramaswamy (2003) 'The new frontier of experience innovation', *MIT Sloan Management Review*, 44(4), pp. 12–18.

9. M. S. OHern and A. Rindfleisch (2010) 'Customer co-creation: a typology and research agenda', *Review of Marketing Research*, 6, pp. 84–106.

10. M. Fisher (2010) *The Co-Production of Social Contagion* (Case Western Reserve University); U. Schultze and A. D. Bhappu (2005) 'Incorporating self-serve technology into co-production designs', *International Journal of e-Collaboration* (IJeC), 1(4), pp. 1–23; R. F. Lusch and S. L. Vargo (2006) *The Service-Dominant Logic of Marketing: Dialog, Debate, and Directions* (ME Sharpe Inc.)

11. N. Franke and E. Von Hippel (2003) 'Satisfying heterogeneous user needs via innovation toolkits: the case of Apache security software', *Research Policy*, 32(7), pp. 1199–215; E. Von Hippel, S. Thomke and M. Sonnack (1999) 'Creating breakthroughs at 3M', *Harvard Business Review*, 77, pp. 47–57.

12. M. E. Adams, G. S. Day and D. Dougherty (1998) 'Enhancing New Product Development Performance: An Organizational Learning Perspective', *Journal of Product Innovation Management*, 15(5), pp. 403–22.

13. ibid.
14. Franke and Von Hippel, 'Satisfying heterogeneous user needs'; Von Hippel et al., 'Creating breakthroughs at 3M'.
15. Fisher, *The Co-Production of Social Contagion*.
16. Fisher, *The Co-Production of Social Contagion*; V. Zwass (2010) 'Co-creation: Toward a taxonomy and an integrated research perspective', *International Journal of Electronic Commerce*, 15(1), pp. 11–48.
17. F. D. Davis (1989) 'Perceived usefulness, perceived ease of use, and user acceptance of information technology', *MIS Quarterly*, pp. 319–40; F. D. Davis, R. P. Bagozzi and P. R. Warshaw (1989) 'User acceptance of computer technology: a comparison of two theoretical models', *Management Science*, 35(8), pp. 982–1003; V. Venkatesh et al. (2003) 'User acceptance of information technology: Toward a unified view', *MIS Quarterly*, pp. 425–78; Y. Malhotra and D. F. Galletta (1999) 'Extending the technology acceptance model to account for social influence: theoretical bases and empirical validation', in *System Sciences, HICSS-32. Proceedings of the 32nd Annual Hawaii International Conference on System Sciences* (IEEE).
18. Davis, 'Perceived usefulness'.
19. United States Census Bureau (2012) *Wholesale & Retail Trade: Motor Vehicle Sales*, p. 663.
20. *iPod Nano Launch* (2010) www.youtube.com: pp. 6–43.
21. Fisher, *The Co-Production of Social Contagion*.
22. Fisher, *The Co-Production of Social Contagion*; Franke and Von Hippel, 'Satisfying heterogeneous user needs'; Von Hippel et al., 'Creating breakthroughs at 3M'; Adams et al., 'Enhancing New Product Development Performance'.

4 THE CONCEPT OF SELF-IDENTITY

1. K. Sharpe (1999) 'Oxytocin Is A Many Splendid Thing: Biochemicals Usurp the Divine', in N. H. Gregersen, U. Görman and C. Wasserman, *The Interplay Between Scientific and Theological Worldviews*, 1, p. 205.
2. L. J. Young (2000) 'Oxytocin and vasopressin as candidate genes for psychiatric disorders: lessons from animal models', *American Journal of Medical Genetics*, 105(1), pp. 53–4.

3. H. J. Lee, A. H. Macbeth and J. H. Pagani (2009) 'Oxytocin: the great facilitator of life', *Progress in Neurobiology*, **88**(2), pp. 127–51.

4. D. Brooks, 'Of human bonding', *The New York Times*, 2 July 2006.

5. T. Hirschi, 'A control theory of delinquency', in (1969) *Criminology Theory: Selected Classic Readings*, pp. 289–305; T. Hirschi (1969) 'Social Control Theory', *Criminology*, pp. 234–7.

6. See, 'Police Say Meth Lab Under Toddler's Bed', http://wreg. com/2013/01/30/police-say-meth-lab-under-toddlers-bed/

7. N. A. Christakis and J. H. Fowler (2009) *Connected: The Surprising Power of our Social Networks and How they Shape our Lives* (Little, Brown).

8. M. J. Hindelang (1973) 'Causes of delinquency: A partial replication and extension', *Social Problems*, pp. 471–87.

9. Marcus Luttrell and Patrick Robinson (2007) *Lone Survivor: The Eyewitness Account of Operation Redwing and the Lost Heroes of SEAL Team 10* (Little, Brown).

10. See NavySeals.com, 'SEAL Code: A Warrior Creed', http://navyseals. com/nsw/seal-code-warrior-creed/

11. T. E. Seeman (1996) 'Social ties and health: The benefits of social integration', *Annals of Epidemiology*, **6**(5), pp. 442–51.

12. E. Durkheim (1951) *Suicide: a Study in Sociology* [1897], translated by J. A. Spaulding and G. Simpson (The Free Press).

13. H. Markus and P. Nurius (1986) 'Possible selves', *American Psychologist*, **41**(9), p. 954–69; H. Markus and E. Wurf (1987) 'The dynamic self-concept: A social psychological perspective', *Annual Review of Psychology*, **38**(1), pp. 299–337; F. Rhodewalt, 'Self-presentation and the phenomenal self: On the stability and malleability of self-conceptions', in (1986) R. F. Baumeister (ed.) *Public Self and Private Self* (New York: Springer-Verlag) pp. 117–42.

14. S. Aral and D. Walker (2010) 'Creating Social Contagion through Viral Product Design: A Randomized Trial of Peer Influence in Networks', Paper 44, ICIS 2010 Proceedings.

15. H. Blumer (1969) *Symbolic Interactionism* (Englewood Cliffs).

16. W. B. Swann and C. A. Hill (1982) 'When our identities are mistaken: Reaffirming self-conceptions through social interaction', *Journal of Personality and Social Psychology*, **43**(1), p. 59.

5   IDENTITY AND SELF-VERIFICATION

1. S. M. Thatcher and X. Zhu (2006) 'Changing identities in a changing workplace: Identification, identity enactment, self-verification, and telecommuting', *Academy of Management Review*, 31(4): pp. 1076–88.
2. S. Stryker and P. J. Burke (2000) 'The past, present, and future of an identity theory', *Social Psychology Quarterly*, pp. 284–97.
3. Thatcher and Zhu, 'Changing identities'.
4. W. B. Swann Jr (1983) 'Self-verification: Bringing social reality into harmony with the self', *Psychological Perspectives on the Self*, 2: pp. 33–66; W. B. Swann Jr, P. J. Rentfrow and J. S. Guinn (2003) *Self-verification: The Search for Coherence. Handbook of Self and Identity*, pp. 367–83.
5. ibid.
6. Swann Jr, 'Self-verification: Bringing social reality into harmony with the self'; Swann Jr, P. J. et al., *Self-verification: The search for coherence*.
7. Swann Jr, 'Self-verification: Bringing social reality into harmony with the self'.
8. Thatcher and Zhu, 'Changing identities'.
9. Swann Jr et al., *Self-verification: The search for coherence*.
10. E. Ries (2011) The Lean Startup (Crown Business).
11. E. Von Hippel, S. Thomke and M. Sonnack (1999) 'Creating breakthroughs at 3M', *Harvard Business Review*, 77, pp. 47–57.
12. J. Surowiecki (2005) *The Wisdom of Crowds* (Anchor).
13. G. Stald (2007) *Mobile Identity: Youth, Identity, and Mobile Communication Media*, The John D. and Catherine T. MacArthur Foundation Series on Digital Media and Learning, pp. 143–64.
14. Unknown (2008) 'Lose Your Cell Phone and You Lose Yourself', *The Miami Student*, (University of Miami Ohio).
15. Stald, *Mobile identity*; Unknown, 'Lose Your Cell Phone'.
16. P. S. Alexander (2000) 'Teens and mobile phones growing-up together: Understanding the reciprocal influences on the development of identity' in *Wireless World Workshop* (University of Surrey).
17. K. A. Bollen (1998) *Structural equation models* (Wiley Online Library).
18. R. Kline (2011) 'Assumptions in structural equation modeling', in R. Hoyle (ed.) *Handbook of Structural Equation Modeling* (New York: Guilford Press).

6   SEEING AND BEING SEEN

1. D. A. Norman (2007) *Emotional Design: Why We Love (or Hate) Everyday Things* (Basic Books), p. 53.

2. W. J. McGuire (1984) 'Search for the self: Going beyond self-esteem and the reactive self', *Personality and the Prediction of Behavior*, **73**, p. 120.

3. H. Dittmar (1992) 'Perceived material wealth and first impressions', *British Journal of Social Psychology*, **31**(4), pp. 379–91; R. W. Belk (1988) 'Possessions and the extended self', *Journal of Consumer Research*, pp. 139–68.

4. J. O'Shaughnessy and N. J. O'Shaughnessy (2002) 'Marketing, the consumer society and hedonism', *European Journal of Marketing*, **36**(5/6), pp. 524–47.

5. R. L. Oliver (1999) 'Whence consumer loyalty?', *The Journal of Marketing*, pp. 33–44.

6. P. Eisler (1997) 'When your team takes a tumble, Guys go awry over losing', *USA Today*.

7. S. Schriver (1997) 'Customer loyalty: Going, going', *American Demographics*, **19**(9), pp. 20–3.

8. E. Sivadas and J. L. Baker-Prewitt (2000) 'An examination of the relationship between service quality, customer satisfaction, and store loyalty', *International Journal of Retail & Distribution Management*, **28**(2), pp. 73–82.

9. A. Tapp (2004) 'The loyalty of football fans. We'll support you evermore?', *The Journal of Database Marketing & Customer Strategy Management*, **11**(3), pp. 203–15.

10. Tapp, 'The loyalty of football fans'.

11. R. W. Pimentel and K.E. Reynolds (2004) 'A model for consumer devotion: affective commitment with proactive sustaining behaviors', *Academy of Marketing Science Review*, **5**(1); C. M. End et al. (2002) 'Identifying With Winners: A Reexamination of Sport Fans' Tendency to BIRG', *Journal of Applied Social Psychology*, **32**(5), pp. 1017–30.

12. See Bleacher Report, 'The Craziest Sports Fans Ever', http://bleacherreport.com/articles/1049509–50–craziest–sports–fans–ever

13. See SFGate 49ers, 'Kyle Williams receiving death threats after NFC Championship', http://blog.sfgate.com/49ers/2012/01/23/kyle-williams–receiving–death–threats–after–nfc–championship/

14. See, Daily Motion, http://www.dailymotion.com/video/xajo17_saturn–vs–spartak–moscow–fan–penalt_sport#.URKmEFr Hd–M

15. See The Off Side, http://www.theoffside.com/world–football/brazilian–fan–threatens–suicide–after–relegation.html

16. See Goal, http://www.goal.com/en/news/9/england/2009/05/06/1249557/kenyan–fan–commits–suicide–after–arsenals–champions–league–defea

17. H. Blumer (1969) 'Social movements', *Studies in Social Movements: A Social Psychological Perspective*, pp. 8–29.

18. E. R. Hirt et al. (1992) 'Costs and benefits of allegiance: Changes in fans' self-ascribed competencies after team victory versus defeat', *Journal of Personality and Social Psychology*, 63(5), p. 724; D. L. Wann and N. R. Branscombe (1990) 'Die-hard and fair-weather fans: Effects of identification on BIRGing and CORFing tendencies', *Journal of Sport & Social Issues*, 14(2), pp. 103–17.

19. R. B. Cialdini et al. (1976) 'Basking in reflected glory: Three (football) field studies', *Journal of Personality and Social Psychology*, 34(3), p. 366.

20. T. Esch and G. B. Stefano (2005) 'The neurobiology of love', *Neuroendocrinology Letters*, 26(3), pp. 175–92.

21. J. A. Peterson and R. Martens (1972) 'Success and residential affiliation as determinants of team cohesiveness', *Research Quarterly*, 43(1), pp. 62–76.

22. D. A. Snow and P. E. Oliver (1995) 'Social movements and collective behavior: Social psychological dimensions and considerations', *Sociological Perspectives on Social Psychology*, pp. 571–99.

23. See H-D History, http://www.harley-davidson.com/en_US/Content/Pages/HD_Museum/explore/hd-history.html

24. See HotBike, 'American Machine Foundry – Journey Into History', http://www.hotbikeweb.com/features/0701_hbkp_american_machine_foundry/

25. See Harley-Davidson, Community, http://www.harley-davidson.com/en_US/Content/Pages/Community/community.html?locale=en_US&bmLocale=en_US

26. J. W. Schouten and J. H. McAlexander (1995) 'Subcultures of consumption: An ethnography of the new bikers', *Journal of Consumer Research*, pp. 43–61.

27. R. Clifton (2004) *Brands and Branding* (John Wiley & Sons).

28. B. Deutsch (2010) 'Luxury products or luxury experiences? Let me tell you a story...', *Luxury Society*, 24 Aug. 2010.
29. L. Mannetti, A. Pierro and S. Livi (2002) 'Explaining Consumer Conduct: From Planned to Self-Expressive Behavior', *Journal of Applied Social Psychology*, **32**(7), pp. 1431–51.
30. W. James (1890) *Principles of Psychology* (University of Chicago Press).
31. Belk, 'Possessions'.
32. M. Featherstone (2000) 'Body modification: An introduction', *Body Modification*, p. 11.
33. See Statistic Brain, http://www.statisticbrain.com/tattoo–statistics/
34. See MeDermis Laser Clinic, http://www.medermislaserclinic.com/free–tattoo–infographic/
35. M. L. Armstrong et al. (1996) 'Motivation for tattoo removal', *Archives of Dermatology*, **132**(4), p. 412.
36. D. Hakim, 'Selling the Sizzle', *The New York Times*, 9 July 2005.
37. R. A. Lutz (1998) *Guts: The Seven Laws of Business that Made Chrysler the World's Hottest Car Company* (Wiley).
38. *Automotive News* (2004) 'U.S. Car Sales, December and 12 Months 2003', Crain Communications, Detroit.
39. C. Isidore, 'GM: Hybrid Cars Make No Sense', CNN/Money Online, 6 Jan. 2004, http://money.cnn.com/2004/01/06/pf/autos/detroit_gm_hybrids/
40. *Automotive News* (2005) 'U.S. Car Sales, December and 12 Months 2004'. Crain Communications, Detroit.
41. C. Isidore, 'Detroit Learning to Love Hybrids', CNN/Money Online, 12 Jan. 2005, http://money.cnn.com/2005/01/12/pf/autos/autoshow_hybrids/
42. C. Calvert (2004) *Voyeur Nation: Media, Privacy, and Peering in Modern Culture* (Basic Books).
43. S. Harris and E. Gerich (1996) 'Retiring the NSFNET Backbone Service: Chronicling the End of an Era', *Connexions*, **10**.
44. See Facebook, Key Facts, http://newsroom.fb.com/Key–Facts
45. D. Ariely, 'How Online Companies Get You to Share More and Spend More', *Wired Magazine*, 20 June 2011.
46. S. D. Gosling et al. (2002) 'A room with a cue: personality judgments based on offices and bedrooms', *Journal of Personality and Social Psychology*, **82**(3), p. 379.
47. L. Nakamura (2002) *Cybertypes: Race, ethnicity, and identity on the Internet* (Psychology Press).

48. Calvert, *Voyeur Nation*.
49. M. Jones (2010) 'Mediated Exhibitionism: The Naked Body in Performance and Virtual Space', *Sexuality & Culture*, 14(4), p. 262.
50. American Psychiatric Association (2000) *Diagnostic and Statistical Manual of Mental Disorders: DSM–IV–TR* (American Psychiatric Publishing).
51. Calvert, *Voyeur Nation*, p. 2.
52. M. Fisher et al. (2011) 'The Co–production of Social Contagion: A Comparative Analysis of Two Social Networking Sites', in *Academy of Management OCIS E–commerce and Service Innovation, Session 2011*.
53. A. Munar (2010) 'Digital Exhibitionism: The Age of Exposure', *Culture Unbound: Journal of Current Cultural Research*, 4, p. 401.
54. H. Koskela (2002) 'Webcams, TV shows and mobile phones: Empowering exhibitionism', *Surveillance & Society*, 2(2/3), pp. 199–215.
55. F. D. Davis (1989) 'Perceived usefulness, perceived ease of use, and user acceptance of information technology', *MIS Quarterly*, pp. 319–40.
56. M. E. Adams, G. S. Day and D. Dougherty (1998) 'Enhancing New Product Development Performance: An Organizational Learning Perspective', *Journal of Product Innovation Management*, 15(5), p. 403–22.
57. E. Von Hippel, S. Thomke and M. Sonnack (1999) 'Creating breakthroughs at 3M', *Harvard Business Review*, 77, pp. 47–57.

7 GETTING IT RIGHT

1. Fritz and Stephen weren't the first to display this violent chemical reaction to the world – they just appear to be the first to do so in an era with the technology to support the viral propagation and consumption of the performance. The first televised performance we could find is credited to retired chemistry teacher, Lee Marek, on the *Late Show* with David Letterman in 1999.
2. See EepyBird at TEDxDirigo, http://www.eepybird.com/featured-video/tedxdirigo/
3. F.Grobe and S. Voltz (2012) *The Viral Video Manifesto: Why Everything You Know is Wrong and How to Do What Really Works* (McGraw-Hill).

4. See Disneyland Musical Marriage Proposal, http://www.youtube.com/watch?v=IpojZ0COU3Y

5. See JK Wedding Entrance Dance, http://www.youtube.com/watch?v=4-94JhLEiN0

6. See http://blogs.thetimes.co.za/gatherer/2009/07/25/kevin-marries-jill—-and-its-the-best-wedding-march-ever/ and http://knowyourmeme.com/memes/jk-wedding-entrance-dance

7. See JK Divorce Entrance Dance, http://www.youtube.com/watch?v=zbr2ao86ww0

8. See 'Norwegian Newspaper Sunmørsposten does JK Wedding Dance', http://www.youtube.com/watch?v=G7xvj_KfEqI

9. T. S. Coffey (2008) 'Diet Coke and Mentos: What is really behind this physical reaction?', *American Journal of Physics*, 76, p. 556.

10. Compete (2009) *Snapshot of Facebook.com*, Compete.com.

11. L. Backstrom (2011) 'Anatomy of Facebook', [cited 15 July 15 2013], available from https://www.facebook.com/notes/facebook-data-team/anatomy-of-facebook/10150388519243859.

12. E. Eldon (2008) '2008 growth puts Facebook in better position to make money', *VentureBeat*.

13. P. Corbett (2009) *2009 Facebook Demographics and Statistics Report: 276% Growth in 35–54 Year Old Users*, iStrategyLabs.

14. '55% of Americans 45–54 now have a profile on a SNS', http://www.socialnomics.net/2012/06/06/10-new-2012-social-media-stats-wow/

15. Backstrom, 'Anatomy of Facebook'

16. Calculated for the month of January 2012, http://www.mediabistro.com/alltwitter/social-media-minutes_b19034

17. Data from Ben Foster, http://www.benphoster.com/facebook-user-growth-chart-2004-2010/

18. A. Johns, 'What are Some Decisions Made by the "Growth Team" at Facebook that Helped Facebook Reach 500 Million Users?' *Slate 2012* [cited 14 Sept. 2012]; Andy Johns was Product Manager, User Growth, at Facebook, 2008–10. Available from: http://www.slate.com/blogs/quora/2012/05/18/team_at_facebook_that_helped_facebook_reach_500_million_users_.html

19. Facebook's 'Find Friends' application, http://www.facebook.com/find-friends

20. Facebook's Privacy Policy – Full Version, http://www.facebook.com/note.php?note_id=%20322194465300

21. Webdesign Tuts+, 'A Brief History on the UI Design of Facebook', http://webdesign.tutsplus.com/tutorials/htmlcss-tutorials/design-and-code-an-integrated-facebook-app-theory/

22. The Facebook Blog, 'Responding to Your Feedback', http://blog.facebook.com/blog.php?post=62368742130

23. Claire Cain Miller, 'Why Twitter's C.E.O. Demoted Himself', *The New York Times*, 31 Oct. 2010, http://www.nytimes.com/2010/10/31/technology/31ev.html?_r=0

24. See Pew Internet, 'Twitter Use 2012', http://pewinternet.org/Reports/2012/Twitter-Use-2012.aspx

25. See Gawker, 'Twitter blows up at SXSW Conference', http://gawker.com/243634/twitter-blows-up-at-sxsw-conference?tag=technextbigthing

26. A. Ostrow (2009) 'Twitter and Facebook Post Huge Growth Numbers in March', [cited 25 Feb 2012], available from: http://mashable.com/2009/04/06/twitter-and-facebook-post-huge-growth-numbers-in-march/

27. See Compete.com, 'Social Networks: Facebook Takes Over Top Spot, Twitter Climbs', http://blog.compete.com/2009/02/09/facebook-myspace-twitter-social-network/

28. See BBC, 'Web slows after Jackson's death', 26 June 2009, http://news.bbc.co.uk/2/hi/technology/8120324.stm

29. See SourceWatch, 'Arab Spring', http://www.sourcewatch.org/index.php?title=Arab_Spring and Wikipedia, *Arab Spring*, http://en.wikipedia.org/wiki/Arab_Spring

30. See Marxist, 'The earthquake', http://www.marxist.com/tunisia-protests-continue.htm

31. See Pacific Standard, 'The Arab Spring's Cascading Effects', http://www.psmag.com/politics/the-cascading-effects-of-the-arab-spring-28575/

32. C. Huang (2011) 'Facebook and Twitter key to Arab Spring uprisings: report', *The National*, Abu Dhabi Media, 6.

33. See TED, 'Evan Williams on listening to Twitter users', http://www.ted.com/talks/view/lang/en/id/473, Feb 2009.

34. See Massively, 'MMObility: How Facebook's recent changes affect MMOs', 14 Dec. 2012, http://massively.joystiq.com/2012/12/14/mmobility-facebooks-recent-changes-and-how-it-affects-mmos/

35. See Switched, 'Facebook reveals its crazy usage figures. FarmVille more popular than Twitter', http://downloadsquad.switched.com/2009/12/03/facebook-reveals-its-crazy-usage-figures-farmville-more-popular/

36. See Gamasutra, 'Phrases Overtakes FarmVille As Top Facebook App', http://www.gamasutra.com/view/news/31675/Phrases_Overtakes_ FarmVille_As_Top_Facebook_App.php

37. See FarmVilleFeed, 'Changes To Facebook News Feeds, Ack Noes!', http://farmvillefeed.com/changes-to-facebook-news-feeds-ack-noes

38. See Games.com, 'Have Facebook's platform policy changes killed free cash promotions?', http://blog.games.com/2011/08/12/ facebook-platform-policy-changes/

39. See *Manchester Evening News*, 'Jailed: Knife killer who stole to play 'Farmville' game on Facebook', 31 Aug. 2011, http://www. manchestereveningnews.co.uk/news/local-news/jailed-knife-killer-who-stole-869569

40. See *Wall Street Journal*, 'How Big Data Is Changing the Whole Equation for Business', 8 March 2013, http://online.wsj.com/article/ SB10001424127887324178904578340071261396666.html

41. See Zynga, 'The FarmVille 2 Almanac of Records and Facts', http://blog.zynga.com/2013/01/04/farmville2infographic/

42. See Seeking Alpha, 'Zynga 4Q12: Farmville 2 Surprises, Mobile Monetization Shows Promise', http://seekingalpha. com/article/1159801-zynga-4q12-farmville-2-surprises-mobile-monetization-shows-promise

43. Reproduced with permission of CSI © 2009. Data Source: CSI www.csidata.com/

44. See NPR, *The Toll of War*, http://www.npr.org/news/specials/tollof-war/tollofwarmain.html

45. See Tripwire Interactive, 'U.S. Spending Billions More, Sending in Fresh Platoons of Experts to Stop IEDs in Iraq', http://forums. tripwireinteractive.com/showthread.php?t=2723

46. JIEDDO, https://www.jieddo.mil/about.aspx

47. FreeRepublic, 'U.S. soldiers use "Silly String" to detect IEDs', 18 May 2007, http://www.freerepublic.com/focus/f-news/1835815/ posts

48. Wikipedia, 'Silly String', http://en.wikipedia.org/wiki/Silly_String

49. Silly String, http://www.silly-string.com/silly-info/silly-string-news.cfm

50. *NY Daily News*, '80,000 cans of Silly String collected, sent to troops in Iraq', 16 Oct. 2007, http://www.nydailynews.com/ news/80-000-cans-silly-string-collected-troops-iraq-article-1.230724

51. FreeRepublic, 'U.S. soldiers use "Silly String" to detect IEDs'.
52. See Michigan Live, 'Jared the Subway Guy tells kids weight gain all started with video games in third grade', 11 Sept. 2012, http://www.mlive.com/living/grand-rapids/index.ssf/2012/09/jared_the_subway_guy_tells_kid.html
53. See Franchise Interviews, 'Jared Fogel – The Subway Diet Story!', http://franchiseinterviews.com/id104.html
54. See Indiana Daily Student, 'Subway's Jared Fogle speaks in Bloomington', http://www.idsnews.com/news/NewStoryPrint.aspx?id=50103
55. D. Swierczynski, 'Stupid Diets...That Work!', Nov. 1999, *Men's Health*.
56. *Post and Courier*, 'All Subways soon will be serving breakfast', http://www.postandcourier.com/article/20100326/PC05/303269969
57. C. Heath and D. Heath (2007) *Made to Stick: Why Some Ideas Survive and Others Die* (Random House).
58. *Commonwealth Journal*, '"Subway Guy" Visits Somerset', http://somerset-kentucky.com/local/x681549706/-Subway-Guy-Visits-Somerset
59. Emily Bryson York, 'Subway Can't Stop Jonesing for Jared', *Advertising Age*, 18 Feb 2008, http://adage.com/article/news/subway-stop-jonesing-jared/125142/

8   GETTING IT WRONG

1. The Onion's Lost Friendster Video, 2009, http://www.youtube.com/watch?v=z9c_1V_eTlw
2. M. J. Piskorski and C.-I. Knoop *Friendster (A)*. Harvard Business School Case Study, 2007(9-707-409).
3. ibid.
4. ibid.
5. ibid.
6. G. Rivlin, 'Wallflower at the Web Party', *The New York Times*, 15 Oct. 2006
7. ibid.
8. M. Chafkin, 'How to Kill a Great Idea!', Inc.com, 1 June 2007, available from: http://www.inc.com/magazine/20070601/features-how-to-kill-a-great-idea.html.

9. ibid.
10. ibid.
11. Piskorski and Knoop, *Friendster (A)*.
12. ibid.
13. ibid.
14. ibid.
15. M. L. Abbott and M. T. Fisher (2010) *The Art of Scalability: Scalable Web Architecture, Processes, and Organizations for the Modern Enterprise* (Addison-Wesley Professional).
16. ibid.; M. L. Abbott and M. T. Fisher (2011) *Scalability Rules: 50 Principles for Scaling Web Sites* (Addison-Wesley Professional).
17. Abbott and Fisher, *The Art of Scalability*.
18. ibid.
19. J.-C. Lin, and L. Hsipeng (2000) 'Towards an understanding of the behavioural intention to use a web site', *International Journal of Information Management*, 20(3), pp. 197–208.
20. Abbott and Fisher, *The Art of Scalability*.
21. ibid.
22. K. Mieszkowski (2003) 'Faking out Friendster' [cited 27 March 2013], available from: http://www.salon.com/2003/08/14/fakesters/
23. ibid.
24. ibid.
25. ibid.
26. ibid.
27. L. Anderson (2003) 'Attack of the Smartasses', *SFWeekly.com*.
28. Piskorski and Knoop, *Friendster (A)*.
29. ibid.
30. ibid.
31. ibid.
32. Chafkin, 'How to Kill a Great Idea!'
33. Piskorski and Knoop, *Friendster (A)*.
34. ibid.
35. ibid.
36. ibid.
37. M. Galehouse, 'Jose Avila's FedEx Furniture Chic', *AZCentral*, 2005, www.azcentral.com
38. K. Philipkoski, 'Furniture Causes FedEx Fits', *Wired* Magazine, 2005, www.wired.com
39. FedEx, 'FedEx Innovation' [cited 27 March 2013], About FedEx, available from: http://about.van.fedex.com/fedex-innovation

9 CONCLUSION

1. M. Benioff and C. Adler (2009) *Behind the Cloud: The Untold Story of How Salesforce. com Went from Idea to Billion-Dollar Company — and Revolutionized an Industry* (Jossey-Bass).
2. G. A. Moore (1991) *Crossing the Chasm* (New York: Harper Business).
3. R. E. Levitt et al. (2011) 'Salesforce.Com: The Development Dilemma', Case study distributed by Collaboratory for Research on Global Projects.
4. See YouTube, Small & Medium Business Product Keynote, http://www.youtube.com/watch?list=PLScnZWsj0lrR0RQWZ1_ENzMjhKkZTY64h
5. See Forbes.com, 'The Ten Most Innovative Companies In America', http://www.forbes.com/sites/samanthasharf/2012/09/05/the-ten-most-innovative-companies-in-america/
6. See http://youtube.com/watch?v=kcWcnFcVRkU
7. G. Hertel, S. Niedner and S. Herrmann (2003) 'Motivation of software developers in Open Source projects: an Internet-based survey of contributors to the Linux kernel', *Research Policy*, 32(7), pp. 1159–77.
8. See http://www.salesforce.com/company/news-press/press-releases/2009/11/091118.jsp
9. See TechCrunch, 'Primary Interface For Salesforce, A Bold Yet Risky Move', http://techcrunch.com/2013/03/22/ceo-marc-benioff-says-chatter-will-become-primary-interface-for-salesforce-a-bold-yet-risky-move/
10. M. Arrington (2006) 'Google Has Acquired YouTube', *Techcrunch*, www.techcrunch.com.
11. E. Lee, 'Google moves Youtube ahead', *San Francisco Chronicle*, 4 March 2007.
12. P. Kafka, 'YouTube's Gigantic Year is Already Here, Citi Says', AllThingsD, 2012.
13. A standard that provides information on human-centered usability methods that can be used for design and evaluation, see http://www.iso.org/iso/catalogue_detail?csnumber=31176
14. A multi-part standard that covers a number of aspects of people working with computers, see http://www.iso.org/iso/home/store/catalogue_tc/catalogue_detail.htm?csnumber=53590

15. A. M. Lund (1997) 'Expert ratings of usability maxims', *Ergonomics in Design: The Quarterly of Human Factors Applications*, 5(3), pp. 15–20.
16. See https://www.hfes.org//Web/Default.aspx
17. See http://www.sigchi.org/
18. See Google's Website Optimizer, http://services.google.com/websiteoptimizer/
19. See Agile product development methodology, http://agilemanifesto.org/
20. See 'Lean Startup', by Eric Ries, http://theleanstartup.com/

APPENDIX A: VIRAL GROWTH

1. H. J. Jones (2007) *Notes on R_0*, Tech. report (Department of Anthropological Sciences, Stanford University).
2. L. Perez and S. Dragicevic (2009) 'An agent-based approach for modeling dynamics of contagious disease spread', *International Journal of Health Geographics*, 8, p. 50.
3. G. Sertsou et al. (2006) 'Key transmission parameters of an institutional outbreak during the 1918 influenza pandemic estimated by mathematical modelling', *Theoretical Biology and Medical Modelling*, 3, p. 38.
4. P. Y. Chen and L.M. Hitt (2003) 'Measuring switching costs and the determinants of customer retention in Internet-enabled businesses: A study of the online brokerage industry'. *Information Systems Research*, 13(3), pp. 255–74.
5. Mathematically, a Pareto distribution is a distribution where there must exist a number (k) such that k% is produced or consumed by $(100 - k)\%$ of the people, items, events, etc. The Pareto principle is commonly used as a rule of thumb to express such things as revenue by sales staff, e.g. 80% of your revenue is produced by 20% of your sales staff.

APPENDIX B: A SHORT SUMMARY OF RESEARCH INFORMING THE BOOK FINDINGS

1. S. Gorard and C. Taylor (2004) *Combining Methods in Educational and Social Research* (Open University Press).

2. A. Tashakkori and C. Teddlie (2003) *Handbook of Mixed Methods in Social & Behavioral Research* (Sage Publications).

3. R. B. Johnson, A. J. Onwuegbuzie and L. A. Turner (2007) 'Toward a definition of mixed methods research', *Journal of Mixed Methods Research*, 1(2), p. 123.

4. Tashakkori and Teddlie, *Handbook of mixed methods*; J. C. Greene, V. J. Caracelli and W. F. Graham (1989) 'Toward a conceptual framework for mixed-method evaluation designs', *Educational Evaluation and Policy Analysis*, 11(3), pp. 255–74.

5. D. L. Madey (1982) 'Some benefits of integrating qualitative and quantitative methods in program evaluation, with illustrations', *Educational Evaluation and Policy Analysis*, 4(2), pp. 223–36.

6. Greene et al., 'Toward a conceptual framework', p. 256.

7. S. Mathison (1988) 'Why triangulate?', *Educational Researcher*, 17(2), pp. 13–17; N. K. Denzin (1978) *Sociological Methods: A Sourcebook* (McGraw-Hill).

8. J. W. Creswell et al. (2003) 'Advanced mixed methods research designs', in Tashakkori and Teddlie, *Handbook of Mixed Methods*, pp. 209–40.

9. R. L. Harrison and T. M. Reilly (2011) 'Mixed methods designs in marketing research', *Qualitative Market Research: An International Journal*, 14(1), pp. 7–26.

10. R. B. Johnson and A.J. Onwuegbuzie (2004) 'Mixed methods research: A research paradigm whose time has come', *Educational Researcher*, 33(7), p. 14.

11. A. Strauss and J. Corbin (1990) *Basics of Qualitative Research* (Sage Publications); B. Latour (1987) *Science in Action: How to Follow Scientists and Engineers Through Society* (Harvard University Press); K. Charmaz (2006) *Constructing Grounded Theory: A Practical Guide Through Qualitative Analysis* (Sage Publications).

12. J. M. Morse (1991) 'Approaches to qualitative-quantitative methodological triangulation', *Nursing Research*, 40(2), pp. 120–3.

13. J. W. Creswell et al. (2003) 'Advanced mixed methods research designs', in Tashakkori and Teddlie, *Handbook of Mixed Methods*, pp. 209–40; A. Tashakkori and C. Teddlie (2008) *Foundations of Mixed Methods Research: Integrating Quantitative and Qualitative Approaches in the Social and Behavioral Sciences* (Sage Publications).

14. Strauss and Corbin, *Basics of Qualitative Research*; Latour, *Science in Action*.

15. Strauss and Corbin, *Basics of Qualitative Research*.

16. ibid.
17. According to http://www.ebizmba.com/articles/social-networking-websites
18. J. S. Coleman (1958) 'Relational analysis: the study of social organizations with survey methods', *Human Organization*, 17(4), pp. 28–36.
19. J. F. Hair et al. (2010) *Multivariate Data Analysis*, Vol. 7 (Upper Saddle River, NJ: Prentice Hall).
20. J. C. Anderson and D. W. Gerbing (1988) 'Structural equation modeling in practice: A review and recommended two-step approach', *Psychological Bulletin*, 103(3), p. 411.
21. C. Fornell and D. F. Larcker (1981) 'Evaluating structural equation models with unobservable variables and measurement error', *Journal of Marketing Research*, p. 39–50; C. Fornell, G. J. Tellis and G. M. Zinkhan (1982) 'Validity assessment: A structural equations approach using partial least squares', Proceedings, American Marketing Association Educators' conference.
22. P. M. Podsakoff et al. (2003) 'Common method biases in behavioral research: A critical review of the literature and recommended remedies', *Journal of Applied Psychology*, 88(5), p. 879.
23. P. M. Podsakoff and D. W. Organ (1986) 'Self-reports in organizational research: Problems and prospects', *Journal of Management*, 12(4), pp. 531–44.
24. G. S. Kearns and R. Sabherwal (2007) 'Strategic alignment between business and information technology: A knowledge-based view of behaviors, outcome, and consequences', *Journal of Management Information Systems*, 23(3), pp. 129–62.
25. Hair et al., *Multivariate Data Analysis*, p. 654.
26. J. Arbuckle (2010) *Amos (version 18)* (Chicago, IL: SPSS).
27. L. Hu and P. M. Bentler (1999) 'Cutoff criteria for fit indexes in covariance structure analysis: Conventional criteria versus new alternatives', *Structural Equation Modeling: A Multidisciplinary Journal*, 6(1), pp. 1–55.
28. R. M. Baron and D. A. Kenny (1986) 'The moderator–mediator variable distinction in social psychological research: Conceptual, strategic, and statistical considerations', *Journal of Personality and Social Psychology*, 51(6), p. 1173.
29. K. Preacher and A. Hayes (2008) 'Asymptotic and resampling strategies for assessing and comparing indirect effects in multiple mediator models', *Behavior Research Methods*, 40(3), p. 879.

30. P. E. Shrout and N. Bolger, 'Mediation in experimental and non-experimental studies: New procedures and recommendation', *Psychological Methods*, 7(4), p. 422.

31. T. Fletcher (2006) 'Methods and approaches to assessing distal mediation', Paper presented at the 66th annual meeting of the Academy of Management, Atlanta, GA.

32. This procedure allows us to distinguish among three types of mediated effects: *indirect*, *partial*, and *complete*. Mediated effects (partial/complete) describe the nature of the relationships that exist between X → Y when the direct effect is significant. By contrast, an indirect effect assumes that the direct effect is non-significant.

33. V. Venkatesh and H. Bala (2008) 'Technology acceptance model 3 and a research agenda on interventions', *Decision Sciences*, 39(2), p. 273.

34. J. Cohen (2003) *Applied multiple regression/correlation analysis for the behavioral sciences*. Vol. 1. (Lawrence Erlbaum).

35. T. Hilton and T. Hughes (2008) 'Co-production and co-creation using self service technology: The application of service-dominant logic', in *The Otago Forum 2*, Dunedin, New Zealand; R. Lusch and S. Vargo (2006) *The Service-Dominant Logic of Marketing: Dialog, Debate, and Directions* (ME Sharpe Inc.)

36. C. Calvert (2004) *Voyeur Nation: Media, Privacy, and Peering in Modern Culture* (Basic Books).

Index

ABC Family, 99
Abrams, Jonathan, 26, 118–21, 123–5
adolescence, 63
advertising, 30
Ajzen, Icek, 41
Amazon, 124
Anderson, J. C., 152
animal experiments, 62
anonymity, 68–9
AppExchange, 134, 135
Apple, 46–8, 54, 55, 76, 127
Arab Spring, 104–5
Ariely, Dan, 92
Aristotle, 62–3
Asian Avenue, 91
attachment, 63–4, 66
attitude-behavior theories, 41, 43
automobiles, 89–91
Avila, Jose, 127

Bagozzi, Richard, 43, 45
Beal, George, 37, 38, 40
belief, 63, 65, 66
Belk, R. W., 89
bell curve of technology adoption, 37–8
Benioff, Marc, 130–1, 136
BIRG (Basking In Reflected Glory), 86, 87
blogs, 50
Bohlen, Joe, 37, 38, 40
Bolt, 91
Bouazizi, Mohamed, 104

brands, 83–4, 96
bricolage, 5, 6, 109, 160
brokerage, 49–50
business-to-business (B2B) models, 130–6

cell phones, 75–6, 77, 79, 88–9, 139
Chatter, 135–6
Classmates, 91
Coca-Cola, 98–100, 114
co-creation, 59, 75, 129, 138
    building the viral misbehavior model, 54–5
    definition of, 160
    extended model, 57–8
    FarmVille, 108
    Friendster, 120
    Intuit Live Community, 72, 73
    making use of the model, 141
    mobile phones, 76
    research results, 153, 156–7, 158–9
    Salesforce.com, 134
    self-identity and, 61
    social networking sites, 8
    Twitter, 106
    virtuous cycle of customer misbehavior, 50, 51, 94
Coleman, Ryan, 113
collective identity, 85, 86–7
commitment, 63, 64–5, 66
Confirmatory Factor Analysis (CFA), 152–4

consumers, 83, 85
contagion, 7, 19, 21–2, 143–4
conversion rate, 22, 23–5, 31, 53, 94, 160
co-production, 8–9, 10, 15, 59, 75, 129, 138
   building the viral misbehavior model, 54–5
   definition of, 160
   extended model, 57–8
   FarmVille, 108
   Friendster, 120
   Intuit Live Community, 73–4
   making use of the model, 141
   mobile phones, 76
   research results, 153, 156–7
   Salesforce.com, 134–5
   self-identity and, 61
   Twitter, 106–7
   virtuous cycle of customer misbehavior, 50, 51, 94
Corbin, J., 149, 150
cortisol, 86
costs, 39, 49
Cox, Chris, 103
'Crazy Nastyass Honey Badger' video, 17–18, 22–3
cultural evolution, 20
cumulative users, 23–4, 53, 94
customer relationship management (CRM), 131, 133
customization, 4, 133–4, 141
cycle of customer misbehavior, 50–2, 55, 58, 66, 74–5, 80, 94–6, 124, 138

Davis, Fred, 10–11, 14, 41–2, 45
Dawkins, Richard, 20
decision making, 39, 44

depression, 65, 67
Deutsch, Bob, 88
diffusion of innovations, 34–7, 38–40, 44
digital exhibitionism, 91, 92–3, 96
direct sales, 28
Dorsey, Jack, 103, 106
Dunton, Maryrose, 136
Durkheim, Emile, 65, 67

early adopters, 36, 38, 40, 44
early majority, 38, 40, 44
ease of use, 10–11, 14, 59, 94–5, 129, 138
   building the viral misbehavior model, 54–5
   definition of, 160
   extended model, 57–8
   Facebook, 101–2
   feedback loops, 78, 139
   Friendster, 120, 128
   Intuit Live Community, 72
   making use of the model, 141, 142
   mobile phones, 75–6
   research results, 153, 156–7
   Salesforce.com, 132–3, 135
   Technology Acceptance Model, 41–3
eBay, 1–5, 6, 9, 11, 55–8, 95, 117
   co-creation, 50
   fan-out, 54
   growth-related problems, 107, 124
   new markets, 116
   product development process, 52
   support community, 74–5, 78, 79

technical difficulties, 122
value of used car market, 48–9,
    60
Eepybird, 98–100, 114
Eisler, Peter, 83
Emmanuel, Chris, 26
exhibitionism, 12, 68, 91–3, 96,
    140
    Friendster's failure, 120, 126,
        128
    research results, 153, 156–7,
        158, 159

Facebook, 13, 58, 79, 100–3,
    114, 128
    Arab Spring, 104–5
    co-creation, 50
    'Crazy Nastyass Honey Badger'
        video, 17
    FarmVille, 107–8
    Friendster compared with, 6–7,
        8, 27, 126
    growth-related problems, 107
    monetizing opportunities on, 116
    research methodology, 149–50
    research results, 154–6
    self-identity on, 12, 14–15, 92,
        102, 154–6
    self-verification on, 78
family, 63, 66
fan-out, 22, 31, 53–4, 55, 57, 59,
    94, 130
    definition of, 160
    Facebook, 100–1, 103
    Friendster, 120
    research results, 153, 156–7,
        158, 159
    Salesforce.com, 132
    YouTube, 137
farmers, 34–5, 36–7, 38

FarmVille, 107–9, 114–15
FedEx, 12, 15, 127, 129
feedback, 70–1, 73–4, 76–8, 79,
    81, 95–6, 139
Fishbein, Martin, 41
Fisher, Mike, 6, 8, 69
Fogle, Jared S., 112–14, 115
fraud, 1–2, 5
frequency of use, 23–5, 31, 144
Friend Sense, 30
Friendster, 6–8, 12, 16, 26–7, 58,
    117–26, 128, 149–50, 154–6

games, 107–9
General Motors (GM), 90, 91
Gerbing, D. W., 152
Glass, Noah, 103
Godin, Seth, 127
Goel, Sharad, 30
Goldstein, Daniel, 30
Google, 18, 76, 99, 119, 124, 137
Gordon, Christopher, 17
Gray, Michael, 127
Grobe, Fritz, 98–9
Gross, Neal C., 34–5, 37
group identification, 85, 86–7
growth, see viral growth

Hamnett, Adam, 108
Harley-Davidson, 87–8
Harvard University, 27
hashtags, 105–6
health issues, 65
heterophilous social systems, 40
Hirschi, Travis, 63, 64
HOGs (Harley Owners Groups),
    87–8
homophilous social systems, 40
hormones, 62, 86
hybrid vehicles, 90–1

identity, 14–15, 32, 82–3, 116,
    129, 138–9, 140–2
  automobiles, 89–91
  concept of, 61
  Facebook, 12, 102, 154–6
  FarmVille, 108
  Friendster, 119–20
  HOGs, 87–8
  making use of the model, 141
  material possessions, 82, 83,
    88–9
  reasons for misbehavior, 54
  research results, 157, 158–9
  Salesforce.com, 135
  self-verification, 68–81
  social bonding, 62–7, 96
  social networking sites, 11–12,
    91–3, 147
  sports fans, 83–7
immersed self-identity, 83, 96
implementation cycle, 130
improvised explosive devices
    (IEDs), 109–11, 115
innovation, 6, 9–10
  brokerage, 49–50
  diffusion of, 34–7, 38–40, 44
  internal and external, 4, 52, 59,
    95, 140
  social networking sites, 8
  Technology Acceptance Model,
    43
innovators, 38, 39, 40, 44
intentions, 41, 43
inter-subjectivity, 66
Intuit Live Community, 68–9,
    71–5, 78, 79, 95, 116, 117
investor returns, 26
involvement, 63, 65, 66
Iowa Agricultural Experiment
    Station (IAES), 35

iPod Nano, 46–8, 50–1, 54, 55,
    57–8
isolation, 65, 67
iWatchz, 46–8, 50–1, 54, 55,
    57–8

James, William, 89
JK Wedding video, 99
Jobs, Steve, 46–8, 57, 130–1
Johnson, R. B., 146
Jones, Matthew, 93
Just for Kicks, Inc., 111

Kalyanam, K., 22
Katz, Jeff, 125
Kenny, Charles, 89–90
Kimber, Richard, 27
Kleiber's Law of metabolism, 145
knowledge, 39
Koogle, Tim, 125
Kubxlab, 46–8

laboratory experiments, 62
laggards, 38, 44
late majority, 38, 44
'lead users', 3, 52, 53, 122–4,
    125, 140
Lewis, Spencer, 84
Lindstrom, Kent, 26
LinkedIn, 50, 58, 78
loyalty, 84, 86, 87
Luttrell, Marcus, 64–5
Lutz, Robert, 90, 91
luxury goods, 15, 82, 88–9

managers, 3–4, 5
marketing, 28, 30
market segmentation, 4
market share, 25, 49, 117
mass media, 36, 39

material possessions, 82, 83, 88–9, 92
McDonald's, 99
mediated voyeurism, 93, 96
memes, 20
Mentos, 98–100
Microsoft, 107
misbehavior
  building the viral misbehavior model, 53–6
  definition of, 160
  drivers of, 56–8
  Facebook, 102
  FedEx, 127
  Friendster, 122–4, 128
  identification of, 95, 96, 99–100, 114
  identity as driver of, 69–71
  opportunities from, 116–17
  pitfalls in addressing, 51–3, 59, 60, 95, 123
  reasons for, 10–13
  Subway, 113
  Twitter, 106–7
  use of the term, 5–6
  virtuous cycle of, 50–2, 55, 58, 66, 74–5, 80, 94–6, 124, 138
misuse
  as co-production, 50
  feedback loops, 77–8, 81, 139
  making use of the model, 141
  as source of growth, 6–10
  use of the term, 5–6
  YouTube, 136–7
mixed methods research, 146–9
mobile phones, 75–6, 77, 79, 88–9, 139
Moore, Geoffrey, 40
motivation, 15, 32, 66, 68
MySpace, 7–8, 125, 126, 128

Netscape, 124
'network effects', 129
Norman, Donald, 82
norms, 63, 64, 82

OfficeMax, 99
Omidyar, Pierre, 1, 6
Onwuegbuzie, A. J., 146
open source software, 135
opinion leaders, 39–40
organic growth, 30–1, 138
Otillo, Troy, 68, 69
oxytocin, 62

parents, 63, 75
Pareto Distribution, 144–5
PayPal, 5
peer attachments, 64
perceived ease of use, 10–11, 14, 59, 94–5, 129, 138
  building the viral misbehavior model, 54–5
  definition of, 160
  extended model, 57–8
  Facebook, 101–2
  feedback loops, 78, 139
  Friendster, 120, 128
  Intuit Live Community, 72
  making use of the model, 141, 142
  mobile phones, 75–6
  research results, 153, 156–7
  Salesforce.com, 132–3, 135
  Technology Acceptance Model, 41–3
perceived usefulness, 10–11, 14, 59, 94–5, 129, 138
  building the viral misbehavior model, 54–5
  definition of, 160

perceived usefulness – *continued*
  extended model, 56–8
  Facebook, 102
  feedback loops, 78, 139
  Friendster, 120, 122, 128
  Intuit Live Community, 72
  making use of the model, 142
  mobile phones, 75–6
  research results, 153, 156–7
  Salesforce.com, 132–3, 135
  Technology Acceptance Model,
    41–3
Perfetti Van Melle, 98–100, 114
performance, 42–3
persuasion, 39
Platform as a Service (PaaS), 134
possessions, 82, 83, 88–9, 92
power-law distributions, 20–1
product development, 4, 12–13,
    52, 78–9, 80, 140
products, 18–19, 56, 97, 144
pyramid of viral growth, 11, 12

Quora, 78

Reasoned Action, Theory of, 41,
    44
reflective self-image, 82
religion, 67
research and development, 4
research methodology, 146–54
respect, 64
retention of users, 13, 23–5, 31,
    59, 94, 144
  building the viral misbehavior
    model, 53–4, 55
  Confirmatory Factor Analysis,
    153
  extended model, 57
  Facebook, 100, 103

Friendster, 120
  research results, 156–7, 158,
    159
Ries, Eric, 71
rodent experiments, 62
Rogers, Everett, 36–7, 38–9, 40,
    44, 45
Rothman, Simon, 1–2, 4–5, 6, 9,
    52, 56–7
Rubbermaid, 28, 29
Ryan, Bruce, 34–5, 37

sales cycle, 130
Salesforce.com, 131–6
Sassa, Scott, 125
Schultz, Randall, 42
S-curve of technology adoption,
    36, 131–2, 137, 138
search engine optimization, 30
self-identity, 14–15, 32, 82–3,
    116, 129, 138–9, 140–2
  automobiles, 89–91
  concept of, 61
  definition of, 160
  Facebook, 12, 102, 154–6
  FarmVille, 108
  Friendster, 119–20
  HOGs, 87–8
  making use of the model, 141
  material possessions, 82, 83,
    88–9
  reasons for misbehavior, 54
  research results, 157, 158–9
  Salesforce.com, 135
  self-verification, 68–81
  social bonding, 62–7, 96
  social networking sites, 11–12,
    91–3, 147
  sports fans, 83–7
self-image, 82

self-verification, 15, 68–81,
    119–20, 142
Shriver, Marcelle, 111
Siebel Software, 131, 133
Silly String, 111–12, 115
'Slashdot effect', 23
Slevin, Dennis, 42
Smith, Adam, 64
social bonding, 15, 54, 61, 62–7,
    82–3, 86, 87, 96
Social Bond Theory, 63, 64
social capital, 40, 49
'social cascade', 22
social exchanges, 11–12, 23, 31,
    147
social interaction, 61, 66, 67
social networking sites, 6–8,
    11–12, 26–7, 44
  exhibitionism, 91–3, 96
  feedback loops, 77
  identity and self-verification,
    68, 78
  mobile phones, 76
  'network effects', 129
  research methodology, 147–8,
    149–54
  research results, 154–9
  see also Facebook; Friendster
social systems, 40
'social village' concept, 85
soldiers, 64–5, 109–12, 115
sports fans, 83–7
Stald, Gitte, 75, 76
Stone, Biz, 103
Strauss, A., 149, 150
stress, 86
structural equation modeling
    (SEM), 76, 152, 158
structural symbolic
    interactionism, 70

Subway, 112–14, 115
suicide, 65, 67, 85
Summize, 105–6
support communities, 68–9, 71–5,
    78–9
Surowiecki, James, 72
sustained growth, 23, 27
symbolic interactionism, 66, 70

tattoos, 89
technical difficulties, 121–2, 124,
    128, 133
Technology Acceptance Model
    (TAM), 41–4, 45, 54, 94,
    132, 138, 148, 156, 160
Technology Adoption Lifecycle,
    37–41, 43
Theory of Reasoned Action, 41,
    44
third places, 85
3M, 95, 125
Toyota, 90, 91
Tupperware, 28, 29
TurboTax, 68–9, 71
Turner, L. A., 146
Twitter, 25, 30, 50, 78, 103–7,
    114

uncertainty, 39, 48, 70
usefulness, 10–11, 14, 59, 94–5,
    129, 138
  building the viral misbehavior
    model, 54–5
  definition of, 160
  extended model, 56–8
  Facebook, 102
  feedback loops, 78, 139
  Friendster, 120, 122, 128
  Intuit Live Community, 72
  making use of the model, 142

usefulness – *continued*
  mobile phones, 75–6
  research results, 153, 156–7
  Salesforce.com, 132–3, 135
  Technology Acceptance Model,
    41–3
user-generated content, 50, 80,
    93, 96, 158–9
  see also co-creation
user groups, 133–4, 136

viral coefficient, 13, 22, 24, 30,
    32, 53, 119, 138, 160
viral growth, 6–7, 11, 12–13,
    14–16, 17–33, 129, 137–8
  building the viral misbehavior
    model, 53–6
  business-to-business models,
    130
  components of, 21–5
  contagion, 7, 19, 21–2, 143–4
  definition of, 19–21, 161
  Facebook, 100–1, 102, 103
  FarmVille, 107–8
  feedback loops, 77–8, 81,
    95–6, 139
  Friendster, 119, 120, 122, 128
  identity and self-verification,
    74–5, 80
  key performance indicators,
    139–40
  making use of the model, 141

Pareto Distribution, 144–5
  possible actions, 144
  research methodology, 147–8
  research results, 154–9
  Salesforce.com, 131–2
  Twitter, 25, 106
  viral growth equation, 13,
    23–5, 31, 32, 53, 93–4
virtuous cycle of customer
    misbehavior, 50–2, 55, 58,
    66, 74–5, 80, 94–6, 124, 138
Voltz, Stephen, 98–9
Von Hippel, E., 72, 125
voyeurism, 12, 68, 91, 93, 96,
    102, 140
  Friendster's failure, 120, 126,
    128
  research results, 153, 156–7,
    158, 159

Watts, Duncan, 30
Web 2.0, 9
Wells, H. G., 83
Williams, Evan, 103, 105–6
Williams, Kyle, 84
Wise, Brownie, 28

Yahoo!, 30, 124
YouTube, 13, 15, 17, 104, 136–7

Zuckerberg, Mark, 27, 101
Zynga, 107–9, 110, 114–15